with dogs at the edge of life

with dogs at the edge of life

colin dayan

 COLUMBIA UNIVERSITY PRESS *NEW YORK*

Columbia University Press
Publishers Since 1893
New York   Chichester, West Sussex
cup.columbia.edu

Library of Congress Cataloging-in-Publication Data
Dayan, Colin, author.
    With dogs at the edge of life / Colin Dayan.
        pages cm
    Includes bibliographical references and index.
    ISBN 978-0-231-16712-3 (cloth : alk. paper)
    ISBN 978-0-231-54074-2 (e-book)
    1. Dog owners—Psychology. 2. Dogs—Social aspects—United States.
3. Human-animal relationships—Moral and ethical aspects.
4. Animal welfare—United States. I. Title.

SF422.86.D93 2016
636.7—dc23
                                              2015020789

c 10 9 8 7 6 5 4 3 2 1

COVER DESIGN: Milenda Nan Owk Lee

COVER IMAGE: Frame from Serge Avedikian, *Barking Island* (2010). (Courtesy of
Serge Avedikian, Ron Dyens, and Thomas Azuélos)

In memory of Mehdi (1996–2011)

and for Stella, the dog of my heart

Among the first were the dogs, faithful creatures, which, scattered about on all the roads, yielded their breath with reluctance.

LUCRETIUS, *DE RERUM NATURA*

contents

preface

IN JACQUES COUSTEAU'S *The Silent World*, there is a spectacular scene shot by the young Louis Malle, an episode so gripping that Cousteau partially restaged it. He filmed it again to get it absolutely right. His actors commit a deed so reckless and brutal that to repeat it seems unspeakable: the first time as reality, the second time as cinema.

The crew of the *Calypso*, a handsome group of men, move through the blue of the sea and dive into the unknown, cage an unruly fish that becomes a pet, mess with coral reefs, cavort with various creatures of the deep. One afternoon the propeller of Cousteau's boat wounds a baby whale. Sharks gather and begin their frenzy of consumption. Something crazy possesses the men as they watch the impassioned gorge, and they take revenge in a massacre fiercer than the shark supper itself. Pulling the sharks onto the deck, they stab and hack them with axes until every last one becomes mincemeat. The deck is awash in blood. Immune to guilt following a slaughter managed as efficiently as Odysseus's killing of the suitors, they return to their senses, and hungry, they leave the deck, going below to eat. Only one nonhuman creature remains alive as witness: a dog. The dog looks at them. Then he gets up and walks away. After carnage too atrocious for words, only the dog responds with what we can interpret as spot-on in its gentle, unremitting regard.

We can never know what the dog's exit means, if it means anything at all. I am captivated by the momentous incomprehensibility of this canine presence. It somehow matters so much or not at all that the action is as close as we get to ethical sensibility in the film. Not instrumental in its moralism, but rather another kind of consideration that is not contemptuous or peremptory. In its reticence and muteness pregnant with meaning, the dog regard matters, even though viewers don't know what to make of it.

HERMAN MELVILLE WAS A STERN ETHICIST when it came to humans ravaging the earth and all living things, especially at sea. In "Stubb's Supper," the chapter in *Moby-Dick* that follows the second mate Stubb's killing of a whale, Melville makes sure readers know that cruelty rages in the hands and hearts of humans. No shark gorging can compare with the sacramental supper on the *Pequod*. He turns the partakers of the feast, "the valiant butchers over the deck-table . . . cannibally carving each other's live meat with carving-knives," into sharks. Then he reaches beyond the whale hunt into a metamorphosis that captures the natural history of the Americas, calling these sharks "the invariable outriders of all slave ships crossing the Atlantic."

Readers of Melville know how much he liked dogs to appear either as grounds for comparison or as characters in their own right. They are loyal pets or savage fighters. They may be abandoned and mournful. But in *Moby-Dick* there are no dogs, unless we recognize them as the ultimate term of comparison in the most sentient and mammalian of scenes. Melville lingers for pages on the pods of whales, hovering together in conjugal peace, coming up to the boats as if "household dogs," reveling in "dalliance and delight" before being wantonly slaughtered by Ahab's crew.

I mention Melville here because he has hovered throughout my writing. Along with dogs, he has been the inspiration. He understood how the very forms of speech and heights of artifice went hand in hand with a history of extermination, always masked by the veneer of enlightenment. Never calling for sympathy or sentiment, Melville writes so that his readers must ask, with Cora Diamond in *The Realistic Spirit*, and I paraphrase, "What could we feel if we could feel what we experience sufficiently?" Such feeling demands a radical change in perspective: not only in how we see the world but also in how we read a story.

MOST OF THIS BOOK is in the form of tales: whether those told by the state, by the law, by humane societies, by dog fighters, dog breeders, dog trainers, or by me as I remember and recognize how dogs came into my life. Dogs stand in for a bridge—the bridge that joins persons to things, life to death, both in our nightmares and in our daily lives.

Every group, every culture needs its scapegoat—the sacrifice that bears the sins of the human community on its back. The dog we label "pit bull" holds in its name all manner of canine jowl and stance. Though this dog is the most obvious brunt of human cruelty, every dog, especially any large dog that has not been tailor-made according to the needs of humans, is at risk, whether in public housing or in the co-ops of New York or on the streets of Romania, Turkey, Mongolia, or Detroit, or in the kill shelters of the United States.

In writing this book, I offer another kind of rendition of creaturely experience that upsets the reliable, reasonable, and moral order of things. The tripartite structure is deliberate. I move between obviously disparate points of view and also through multiple identities. Dogs bear the burden of revelation. With them, and succumbing to their gaze, as unintelligible as that of Cousteau's dog, I try to narrow the gap between body and mind, human and nonhuman, matter and spirit.

I do not mean here to call to mind any concept of relativism but rather to cast doubt on the robustness and transportability of the ontological partitions that we so easily assume. This is a personal bias, since I have long tried to invoke, even if tentatively, the seepage between entities assumed to be distinct, whether dead or living, animate or inanimate, commonplace or extraordinary. For me the interstitial, a poise or suspension between opposites, matters most. So I invoke the oscillation between the categories that bind. Such a suspension matters to me both literally and figuratively, as a matter of politics and of aesthetics. The necessity of working in the interstices has been with me for quite some time now, ever since I first read Mallarmé, who tackled the *centre du suspens vibratoire*, or center of vibrating suspension, in pursuit of "pure poetry." Some eighty years later, in calling for a people's revolution, Frantz Fanon summoned *la zone d'instabilité occulte*, the zone of occult instability. From inside this place between poetry and politics, I appeal to a novel textual environment. I want to reshuffle the terms of how we come to know what we cannot know. And out of this desire comes a great deal that is hypothetical or even imaginary. Some events on which I try to focus dissolve, as I track dogs both in and outside of my experience.

So this book invites cohesion between supposedly distinct entities, even genre and voice. Part I, "Like a Dog," is memoir. It was unexpected even to me and took shape in ways I did not anticipate. An attempt to come to terms with the person writing, these pages are also a backward look at how dogs came into focus. Or, to put it more boldly, the question implicit throughout this writing, it now seems to me, must be: Why did they come to mean so much to me, to be the true passion of my life?

Part II, "When Law Comes to Visit," is the oldest, the place where I began. About dogs and the humans who either live for them or kill them, it considers how dogs matter to our sense as social and political animals. I am not interested here in animal rights, in giving animals what we think it is we get as bearers of rights and obligations in standard liberal moral terms. Rather, I examine what happens when the fates of certain kinds of dogs and certain kinds of men intertwine. I am not in an easy position, nor am I sanguine about the consequences of what these chapters yield in the manner of political life. This material—the men and their dogs—rooted as it is in the rural South, will make some of my readers uneasy. The reaction is a good thing, as it is prompted by the brute facts of the cases, most especially when legal logic or our own posture of decency seems to assuage obvious pain and loss.

In trying to characterize the specific landscape of judicial cruelty, I am concerned about the preemptive violence that targets dogs and their owners: the seizures, detentions, and exterminations of so-called pit bulls. Canine profiling supplies the terms for ostracism and suspension of due process rights. No criminal conviction of the owner is required for state seizure of property. In this unholy alliance of intolerance and state power, the specter of forfeiture lives on in the contemporary United States. The Constitution's Fifth and Fourteenth Amendments, which prohibit the government from depriving anyone of "life, liberty, or property, without due process of law," can be—and often are—suspended for the public good without evidence, without trial, by classification alone.

Deprivation and loss, the end to old ways of life, the extremity of suffering experienced by those who live still in the grip of an old faith or traditions, remain central in part III, "Pariah Dogs," which thinks through the cinematic representation of the disposal or extermination of stray dogs. Whether set in the streets of Istanbul or on the steppes of Mongolia, the films I discuss imply something intolerable about progress. In the mercenary pressures of global civilization, the turn to dogs chisels into our consciousness the sensational quality of memory. Through physicality so extreme that it becomes a means of perception, we move forward and backward through time. We are forced to leave ourselves and pass over into something else, different in quality and expression.

Even while we are ostensibly doing everything in our power—whether through canine-focused marketing campaigns or functional magnetic resonance imaging—to ascertain the nature and desires of dogs, the questions we ask sometimes obscure or betray what is most salient about them and necessary to their lives. And through it all, the testing and the loving, the ownership and the training, the argument for dog rights and the facts of their disposal, we never question the status of reason as a problem, not a privilege. It's time to begin to ask what we mean by *human*, to make humanity a position marked by uncertainty. These pages should encourage collision and conflict, the debates that alone can counter the dismal and pernicious (evil because hidden under cover of rationality) effects of a liberal consensus that silences and excludes whatever does not adhere to coercive calls for civility and reasonableness.

I have always thought that morality is not ethics. Moral judgment takes its position from a communal surround of privilege. It depends for its power on the people who ordain right and wrong and on public acquiescence. Ethics takes on for me a meaning that is less abstract. It has to do with locale, the proximity of one creature to the other or how an individual relates to what is not familiar. To be ethical, in this sense, is to locate oneself in relation to a world adamantly not one's own. Whereas morality is an austere experience of nonrelation, ethics demands the discomfort of utter relatedness.

My aim, then, is to prompt another kind of experience that can be felt but not always understood. By concentrating on that aspect of the reader's mind that can perceive but not comprehend, I hope to sharpen the appetite for seeing and knowing, even while suggesting something indiscernible behind what is seen and known. Mood replaces certainty. We are left with an all but unintelligible feeling. Or is it another kind of intelligibility? To lie on the ground with dogs is to think through what an alternative world might look like. In awe of such intimacy—wherever it is found, in the home or the dump—I have written this book.

with dogs at the edge of life

by way of beginning

BEFORE I KNEW WHAT SHAPE this book would take, I wrote a few things that appear to me now like something of a jeremiad. My preoccupation with the surfeit of sociality that I experience with dogs led me to think more and more about the terrain of the rough-hewn and the lost. Emptiness took hold of me, accompanied by a pain or anguish of the heart I had not experienced before. I take these writings to be an appeal to our conscience—not what Reinhold Niebuhr condemned as "the easy conscience of modern man" but rather something more difficult, an experience that radically changes how we see the world. *With Dogs at the Edge of Life* asks us to feel and experience, not only to think.

As I reckon with a manner of introducing this work, I realize that the best way, in the sense of being honest with readers, is to present what I wrote when I first envisioned it. It is as if I draw the curtain open onto the feeling that led me away from what I thought I knew and into a world of submerged memories. That past had always been somewhere in "the dark backward and abysm of time." But it was no Prospero who called me to the task of remembering. Instead, my dogs drew me back to what I had forgotten. They urged me on. And only then did I learn how to live.

I CANNOT SLEEP. The images of the dog on straw, the dog on cement, the dog with something like filth and dust on his head, the dog with clouds for eyes, the dog with hair gone in swirls over his body, leaving white where black had been, the dog with a muzzle covered with pustules, the dog who died on July 10, 2012, killed by the Belfast City Council.

The dog is on my mind, and I cannot fathom how, even in his death, he could not be returned to the family who loved him. Lennox's body was burned to ashes and mailed to the family who never again laid eyes on him after the spring day in 2010 when he was taken away from his home because he was measured and labeled a "pit bull–type dog." For two years the family, with tens of thousands of supporters, fought to save him from confinement and murder.

The annihilation of Lennox, the disposal of his body once dead, alerts us to what is more than just another dog story. We are living in a time of extinctions. And the disposal of Lennox helps us to understand why. Fear is a vice that takes root. Fear and the brutality that accompanies it can be recognized only when the human and animal are brought together, when what yokes us as creatures puts us in the proverbial same boat. Such brutality is not easy to brook.

So how to speak about this commonplace slaughter? Such extermination is a sign not only of our collective cruelty but also of the politics at the core of our twenty-first century. The management of what is deemed refuse distinguishes between the free and the bound, the familiar and the strange, the privileged and the stigmatized. Let us think for a moment about the unreal rationality of a racism that depends for its power on the conceptual force of the superfluous. To be disposable is *not* having the capacity to be dispossessed—to be nothing more than dispensable stuff.

WHEN EVERYTHING HAS BEEN LOST—your job and your home, your possessions—you move on to find work, sometimes taking your dog with you. Last year the *New York Times* reported that many of the families who had recently moved to Wyoming seeking work in the energy industry ended up homeless. They are described as "economic migrants from Florida and Michigan, Wisconsin and California with nowhere to settle." In a country that has labels for people outside the pale of human empathy, this portrayal of those snatched out of their former lives and homes by what the reporter calls a "soured economy" haunts me. The economy is far from sour for the few who live ever more lushly with ever more money in our midst. But what caught me most were the words of Lily Patton, a housing counselor in Natrona County, Wyoming: "They'd pack up their pit bulls, their children and they'd move to Wyoming with nothing, just the clothes on their backs."[1] If we were challenged to write a history of dispossession, we could go to no better place than the foreclosures of an imagined humanity when bounded and sharpened by the dog kind.

> If they do this to anyone who begs,
> drugged, drunk, or sober, with or without legs,
> what would they do to sick, four-leggèd dogs?
> ELIZABETH BISHOP, "PINK DOG"

CITY STREETS ARE SOMETIMES DANGEROUS—if you happen to be poor, black, or a pit bull. Rural areas are sometimes dangerous—if you happen to be poor, white, or a pit bull. This catalog puts in relation humans and dogs in what might seem a tasteless or even racist merging. But the taint of proximity matters.

While the oligarchs and the obscenely wealthy of this country run the show, they make sure that the divide between poor white and poor black is pronounced and spectacular. It is carved into the heart of public life in the United States. Some well-heeled and influential nonprofit organizations stoke that division. There are always racist killer whites, but they are not the majority of the "white trash" in the countryside. Yet the pit bull—targeted and reviled, unless saved by a middle-class urban white—joins whites and blacks in a jagged and unlikely bond.

In April 2009, the New York City Housing Authority (NYCHA) instituted a ban on pit bulls (also identified as Staffordshire terriers), Rottweilers, and Doberman pinschers—"all of these either full breed or mixed breed"—or any full-grown dog weighing more than twenty-five pounds. That means almost any dog bigger than a dachshund or corgi. Tenants feared eviction if they kept their dogs. An exception was made for those registered before the policy was implemented on May 1. But many dog owners weren't notified and learned of the new policy on television or via fliers from community organizations. Some heard nothing at all.

A few days after the ban was announced, a woman named Iris posted a complaint on the blog of the American Society for the Prevention of Cruelty to Animals. She was enraged by what she called "this pit bull discrimination war":

> I got a notice by the new york city housing authority that they are banning pit bulls from public housing. Me and basically all of the people where I live have pit bulls. . . . What I would like to know is if what housing doing legal? And can they do this? . . . They are just basically saying since pit bulls have a reputation as being so called dangerous dogs. That they have to blame all pit bulls. I am not any good at expressing myself in writing. But is there anyone out there that can help me save them from being taken away from loving home.

Five months later, on September 22, the *New York Times* announced on its front page: "Large Dogs in Public Housing Are Now Endangered Species." The article reported that since April at least 113 dogs had been surrendered to shelters run by Animal Care and Control of New York City, a nonprofit group that takes in unwanted animals. "Of the 113 dogs," according to the *Times*, "49 have been euthanized, because of illness, behavior or a lack of space."

The NYCHA considers the possession of large dogs, especially breeds categorized as "dangerous," to be "lease violations" or, with a nod to former mayor Rudolph Giuliani, "Quality of Life infringements or crimes." Dogs left behind in New Orleans after Hurricane Katrina, or taken from the arms of their owners as they got on buses to flee the drowning city, are evidence of the way prejudice against the disenfranchised is made real in the fate of their dogs.[2]

The modern conception of dogs as personal property has done very little to advance their position. They remain subject to the same repressive treatment as others targeted for coercion and control. They have taken their place alongside vagrants and criminals. Out of the maimed right of property in dogs has come a familiar deprivation of persons considered either too servile or too poor to count. The ban not only harms dogs but also further disenfranchises those thought unfit for ownership.

ON APRIL 26, 2012, Maryland's highest court decided in *Tracey v. Solesky* that the American Staffordshire terrier or American pit bull terrier, or any mix containing pit bull genes, is "inherently dangerous" as a matter of law. The ruling followed a case brought by parents whose ten-year-old son was mauled by a pit bull. They sued the dog owner's landlord, but the trial judge threw out the lawsuit, ruling that the landlord had not been proven negligent. The Maryland Court of Appeals then reviewed the case and decided that negligence was not an option. The breed alone would count as evidence that an individual animal is violent, subjecting owners to what the courts call "strict liability." That means that legally, pit bulls are like tigers. To own a pit bull is to live at risk, for liability has nothing to do with fault—or even knowledge of danger—on the part of the owner. From this point on, in Maryland, *any* pit bull would be considered a danger to humans. The appeals court declared, "When an attack involves pit bulls, it is no longer necessary to prove that the particular pit bull or pit bulls are dangerous."[3]

In his dissent, Judge Clayton Greene recognized the absurdity of the majority opinion's "unworkable rule." "How much 'pit bull' must there be in a dog to bring it within the strict liability edict?" he asked. "How will that be determined? What rationale exists for any particular percentage of the genetic code to trigger strict liability?"[4] In the absence of a viable genetic test, so-called experts will instead tell courts that an individual dog either is or is not a pit bull mix, based on nothing more than the shape of its head, or its stance, or its way of looking at you. When psychologists at Case Western Reserve University asked a controlled group of subjects to select pit bulls from a random assortment of dogs, subjects recognized nearly 70 percent of the dogs as pit bulls.[5]

Aileen Gabbey, the executive director of the Maryland SPCA, which is independent of the national organization based in New York, told *Baltimore Sun* columnist Dan Rodricks that she disagreed with the ruling since breed has little to do with a dog's violence. The pit bulls she sees are "victims—abused, forced to fight, given up."[6] The Humane Society also took a stand against the ruling, estimating that it could affect as many as seventy thousand dogs in Maryland. Chief Program & Policy Officer Michael Markarian explained, "This sweeping decision is a case of canine profiling. It may force law-abiding citizens to face a painful and life-changing decision—move out of Maryland or give up their beloved dogs."[7]

Pit bulls have no special characteristic that makes them dangerous. There is no pit bull gene for danger. The consequences of condemning an entire breed in this way soon became obvious. Insurance companies stopped covering places where a pit bull is around. People had either to give up their pets or to lose their homes. Armistead Homes Corporation in Baltimore issued an ultimatum to its low-income residents: they must get rid of their pure and mixed-breed pit bulls or be evicted. After just four and a half months on the books, the pit bull ruling was challenged in federal court when Joseph Weigel, an Armistead Gardens resident, sued the state, asking judges to strike down the court ruling. Weigel's attorney said that as many as five hundred dog owners in Armistead Gardens would be "faced with a very hard choice—homelessness or euthanization of their dogs."[8] On June 19, 2013, the district court granted the state's motion to dismiss the case.

On April 8, 2014, nearly two years after the court validated canine profiling, Governor Martin O'Malley signed the bill that overturned *Tracey v. Solesky*. The bill removed liability for landlords unless the landlord knew that the dog was dangerous. Now owners are liable for injuries caused by their dog, no matter the breed.[9] But what happens in the courts or legislatures has little effect on what happens to these dogs on the streets and in the homes of the United States. Certain kinds of humans and dogs, once labeled as expendable, can be sacrificed to the realities of lawful control.

"OH NO, HE'S SHOOTING THE DOG. Stop shooting." A person on a cell phone is heard as the police in Hawthorne, California, about fifteen miles southwest of downtown Los Angeles, restrain a black man and shoot his dog dead in the light of day. That kind of message is heard again and again in the streets of the United States as police assault, even kill, humans and dogs. In New York in August 2012, police shot a pit bull named Star in the head when he tried to protect his companion, a homeless white man named Lech Stankiewicz. The man had an epileptic fit, and the dog tried to stop the police when one of them kicked Stankiewicz as he lay on the street. We see the police shoot the dog and we see him alone, bleeding in the street not far from the person he protected.

But the episode of the Rottweiler named Max and his owner, Leon Rosby, at the hands of the Hawthorne police, though all too familiar in our cities, is much more disturbing. Caught on video, the fatal shooting on an afternoon in July 2013 is hard to watch. Not once but four times the shots hit the body of the dog. The bullets hit so hard that Max seems to jump, roll, and bounce off the curb as Rosby, handcuffed by police, looks on.

Rosby was walking Max when he saw a SWAT team approaching a house in response to a robbery. Rosby had already filed six complaints against the Hawthorne Police Department, alleging mistreatment and racial profiling. Used to the department's civil rights violations and pattern of intimidating and harassing African Americans, he started to videotape the SWAT team. Officers approached him, and he returned the dog to his car, where music blared from the radio. Rosby walked over to the police. They did not talk; they handcuffed him and roughed him up. As you hear in the video, Max is barking, barking, barking. The dog sees his friend Rosby tackled, manhandled, held by the police. When the police get tougher, Max jumps out the window to protect Rosby. You hear Rosby telling Max to get back. "No, Max!" he calls. Max does not attack the officers. He comes toward them, backs up, and then turns to Rosby. The police start to yell, and another officer comes running over. That policeman shoots the dog not just one time, not just to stop him, but several times, to make sure he is dead. The dog stops after the first bullet. He tries to get away. Three more bullets, and the dog somersaults over the curb and rolls off onto his back. His legs churn the air, like those of a dying roach trying to live.

Rosby never gets to hold his dog again. He is pulled away and shoved into the police car. Care and grief are no longer allowed in this America. "He wasn't just a dog, you know," Rosby said, speaking about Max after the killing. "He'd lick on my face, lick on my ear. . . . The dog wouldn't have lunged at you if you hadn't approached him like that, I know it, I know my dog." Later he explained that his dog "was trying to stop them from beating on me."[10]

As I watched the video, I heard Malcolm X's words from nearly forty years earlier: "If a dog is biting a black man, the black man should kill the dog, whether the dog is a police dog or a hound dog or any kind of dog. If a dog is fixed on a black man when that black man is doing nothing but trying to take advantage of what the government says is supposed to be his, then that black man should kill that dog or any two-legged dog who sicks the dog on him."[11] Nothing seems to enrage police these days more than a black man who owns a dog, and it is worse for the black man who loves a dog. It is almost as if somewhere in the minds of these police they believe that dogs were made for hating blacks, not for loving them. That is the horror and the tragedy caught by Samuel Fuller in his film *White Dog*, adapted from the novel by Romain Gary.

I think about growing up in the South in the 1960s and, closer to home, about my neighborhood in Atlanta where I learned to watch out for the white men in uniforms. They threatened us through our dogs. They were called "the laws" when they weren't called "dog catchers." We never knew the difference between them. Police took away your dogs. Dog catchers picked up dogs in their nets, loaded them into the back of their trucks, and took them to the pound. Both could do whatever they wanted to the dogs and their owners. Theirs was an alternative laying down of the law as old as the day is long. From the days of slavery, through abolition, down to the present, dog catchers have been granted "police power." Anything is permissible as long as it is in the interests of the community: its health, safety, and welfare. That community is still understood to be white and affluent.

If I say that nothing has changed for the majority of blacks in this country, I can back it up with the words: all you have to do is look at the treatment of their dogs. There is the proof. There is the rub. Shooting family pets—especially pit bulls, but any large dog will do—has become a habit, a ritual that reminds citizens of the reach of lawful predation. Whether these are dogs too large to be allowed in public housing or too insignificant to be taken on buses from Hurricane Katrina, whether they are shot dead on the streets or even in the backyards of their homes, is no matter. It is instructive to watch how prejudice works—the one-on-one lamination of the pit bull onto the African American male, the circuitous routes it takes, the consequences of reducing persons to their accessories: you know, it's not the men you're afraid of, it's their dogs.

When I saw the video of Rosby's arrest and Max's murder, I tried to tell my husband the story. The only way to get him to feel the horror was to reenact it. So I became the dog. I barked. I jumped and ran toward my husband. Still barking, I leapt. First, one bullet; then, three more bullets. I did a somersault on the floor of the study and rolled over on my back, my legs in the air. He looked at me in silence. I cried. My dog Stella ran in the room. She came over, laid her body on top of me, both legs and paws pressed on my chest. I was enveloped by her care, her knowledge that something big and awful had just happened to me. She stayed there close and licked my face, tongue hard against my cheeks, with a passion I had not felt in a long time.

HOW CAN I SEIZE ON DOG LIFE IN WORDS? Dogs live on the track between the mental and the physical and sometimes seem to tease out a near-mystical disintegration of the bounds between them. What would it mean to become more like a dog? How might we come up against life as a sensory but not sensible experience? We all experience our dogs' unprecedented and peculiar attentiveness. It comes across as an exuberance borne by a full heart. Perhaps this is what the Puritan divine Jonathan Edwards meant when he emphasized a *physical* rather than *moral* conversion. He knew that the crux of divinity in earthbound entities lay in the heart's "affections."

What does conscience look like at the boundaries of humanity, at the edge of a cherished humanism? The ruses of sentiment fail to confront the alternately knowing and doubting relation that matters most between humans and dogs. What does it mean to think outside our selves and with other beings? For dogs, thought is immersed in matter. Not sympathy or sentiment but something more acute and unsettling. When dogs find themselves in the wrong place at the wrong time, belonging to the wrong kinds of people or protecting too earnestly the homes of their human companions, they gather themselves up in their flesh, and in a state of prescience and acceptance, they prepare for the time when life stops, as they slip away toward stillness. It is not that they do not know what is going to happen to them but that they know too well.

Taking the life, death and even breath of dogs as my prompt, then, I want to unsettle our conceptual schemes in order to examine another way of engaging with other beings. What would it mean to know like a dog? Ultimately it is a question of palpable anticipation, not abstract moralizing. Dogs are not, as Donna Haraway proposes, in a twist on the words of Claude Lévi-Strauss, "here just to think with," but also "here to live with." They might also be the form that thought must take if it is to make a difference to our lives.

Disregard, forfeiture, and extinction. These words can be understood in their reach and dread if we force ourselves to see double: dogs and their not quite kin, the humans with them or against them, loving or hating them. In this time of economic collapse, political paralysis, and continuing race hatred, dogs help us to understand the contemporary mixture of disciplinary and penal power. It is with dogs beside us and before us that we are prompted to reconsider the ethical life: the conscience it demands, the liabilities it incurs. For those of us who believe that the sharp distinction between human and nonhuman animals is unsustainable, this book offers ways of thinking through the making and unmaking of life on this earth.

part one

like a dog

MY LIFE, WHAT I REMEMBER of my childhood, began with a dream. I dreamed that I was in a dump, out there in the dirt with broken footstools, cracked dishes, and piles of toys. No one else was there. I had been dropped off and left alone right before the sun set. I do not remember myself—how I looked, what I felt. All I see even now are things. The things in the dirt are not garbage, not like the stuff you throw in trashcans. They are weighty, extravagant, and intemperate in their height and clutter. That is the feeling I have when I call up the dream. I am there thrown away in a heap, in the midst of junk that, treasured once, still seems effervescent with love, imprudent in excess.

What are the things that get left behind, disposed of, forgotten? In heaps they pile up, one on top of the other, a clutter of dead bodies that somehow hold on to life: in the limb thrown softly onto the back of its neighbor, in the mouths held open, not quite ready to turn away from the life they knew. This held breath, the hot blood and flesh of abandoned stuff, matters to those who live. To know our easy disregard is to hold fast to the sight of what we push aside. Only then do we come to know what we have lost.

In the piles of the dead, things still hold the pulse and beauty of what we claim to cherish but continue to kill.

Dogs are captive in the yoke of care and cruelty that defines our status as humans. They are property and persons, both *res nullius*, or no one's thing, and valuable possession. Our contradictions, inconstancy, and greed continue to make large groups of persons,

 whether human or non-human, expendable. And nowhere is that indignity as clear as in our relation-ship with dogs. Nowhere do we experience so fully the alternating closeness and disregard of those who master—those whose ritu-als of disposal undergird and sustain the soft, clos-eted lives of the privileged.

It is with the dogs that I begin. They are the things of great attachment that can be cast off. Their relentless passion and full heart compel a new understanding of spirit and a new appreciation of flesh. Though blessed, they are also like the junk I dreamed about and into which I was tossed. This book is about what gets treated as refuse, tossed off as trash in the world of high-status human animals. But it is also about the dogs that, in spite of the constant uncertainty of their lives, saved me from the dump, calling me back, again and again, to life.

dogs and light

Deep the woods and dark the scent
As the bright season lengthens
Into the work of the mind for
Which the dogs live
VICKI HEARNE, "NEWS FROM THE DOGS"

A PHILOSOPHER, POET, and professional trainer of horses and dogs, Vicki Hearne died on August 21, 2002. Her husband, Robert Tragesser, sent me the notes to the preface of the posthumously published "Tricks of the Light," the five-part sequence poem that she worked on right up until her death. It was published in the volume of collected poems with the same title. She felt the need to explain her change of muse from horses to dogs:

> But I have outlived and outwritten the ability to invoke exalted horses who outlive or outwrite the ability to send a good or, if the gods should so will a great, dog out into the fields of the imagination, and its forests, its planets.
>
> It is not that no preparation is needed. I have put the supernatural, that is to say, great, dog in the place of the winged horse, and the good dog in the place of the serviceable word.[1]

Her words return dogs to their rightful place as medium of thought and criterion of utterance. Their thought is heavy and palpable as flesh. The sure sign of the spirit, as Saint Paul knew, could be touched, held, and smelled. In "Tricks of the Light" she speaks to and with the dogs. She lets her readers know the stirring of knowledge that is none other than the dog's personal surpassing:

> the dog's leap beyond herself
> and a twirl and flash
> of a toothed belief.[2]

I first met Vicki at Yale. Into the office across from me she brought two pit bulls, Michael and Annie, and two pink plastic chaise lounges. It was the first time I ever saw dogs like them, so intense, focused, and muscular. Vicki's office mate, a non-

dog-loving medievalist, did not welcome them. But who ever expected pit bulls in Linsly-Chittenden Hall? Walking up the stairs with Vicki and her dogs seemed to me a glorious ritual, one of great concentration. I remember feeling as if light shone around their bodies, and I was honored to accompany her and the dogs. Even now I sense the demands of her belief, and I hear her airy gasp that meant a dog was in sight. I held the dumbbell, the choke collar, and the long line, heavy and magical in my hand.

Years later, when I had moved out to the Tucson Mountains in Arizona, Vicki came to visit. By then I had the three dogs of my life: Dogie the Rottweiler, Mehdi the Am Staff, and Jesse the black Labrador. Dogie, the oldest and the largest of the three, never took to training. His trainer became my lover. That probably contributed to his recalcitrance. Or maybe I was just too lax and easygoing. Vicki took Dogie out to the front steps of the house in Tucson. It was hot, it was summer, and she had accepted my love and his bad training. My dog sat, and she put choke collar and long line around his neck. He would not move. There he sat, at the top of the steps. So dragged he was, down the stairs, all 120 pounds, and then he landed flat out on the ground, with Vicki, who joined him there, laughing.

Vicki had no truck with smug oversimplifications or pious surmises based on narrow judgments about victimization and mastery. Claims of humane treatment are not reassuring. Dogs can be killed with kindness. Nothing is more dangerous to their sense of themselves than coddling. The choke collar, used correctly just once, with the impersonality of a force of nature, gives a dog the space in which to focus, to know where and how it wants to be. The annoying sound of the clicker, on the other hand, crowds the dog into acknowledging what it might want to ignore. So one click usually will not do. The bribery of treats follows. This coaxing requires no intimacy between dog and person, no exchange of recognition. Ignored as capable of intent or will, the dog must accept the characterization that remains: nothing more than a creature with an insatiable appetite. So we have Elizabeth Costello's story of Sultan the ape in J. M. Coetzee's *The Lives of Animals*: "At every turn Sultan is driven to think the less interesting thought. From the purity of speculation (Why do men behave like this?) he is relentlessly propelled toward lower, practical, instrumental reason (How does one use this to get that?) and thus toward acceptance of himself as primarily an organism with an appetite that needs to be satisfied."[3]

In *Bandit: Dossier of a Dangerous Dog*, her remarkable story of saving a dog sentenced to death, Vicki describes what happens when people give positive reinforcement, such as biscuits, to teach dogs to sit. Such rewards reduce "the complex of meanings" that a dog can give to the act of sitting. "Continual treat reinforcement of the puppy's sitting discourages the puppy from trying to mean anything but a treat. . . . Truth becomes a dog biscuit, an M&M, a sitcom, or cocaine . . . whether or not the human beings know that in the process they and the dog have lost a language and thus a world."[4]

I remember Vicki's visit to the University of Arizona in 1994, where her words and presence struck terror in the hearts of many dog-loving professors in the audience. She urged that the character and responsibility earned through absolute obedience to the craft of training give dogs both a language and a presence squarely in the world. My colleagues complained: "Her use of force is fascist." One woman boasted, "I use a clicker to show my dog who is boss." That evening at a cocktail party, Vicki, who dared take out a cigarette, was told to go outside. Ignored by everyone, there she stood for the next few hours, alone, in the desert on a terrace under the stars. She had been banished, I thought. Vicki had stamped in hunger for the word, sweated to the cadence of reflection, and beaten out thought in brutal prose. The promise of language and the rapture of thought held always tight in the leap, the retrieval, the tracking of dogs. So she writes of dog knowledge, learning at the edges of work in "Tricks of the Light":

> Proof is all in the mind,
> the mind is all in the world,
> the world is a star
>
> caught in a young bitch's teeth
>
> just as she is learning the grab
> of the heart that sends her past hurt
>
> into her work, leaving doubt
> in the dust of regret
> that stains the bureaucrat's breath.[5]

In our decent and all-too-human times, Peter Singer argues for the sanctity of animal life by making an analogy between animals and the incapacitated and insane. Since animals suffer and feel pain like these disabled humans but have the added ingredient of reason, even if limited, they deserve to occupy a place of rights as "non-human persons."[6] The horror of drug testing on dogs and cats, of the care and stuffing of cows or chickens, pigs or sheep, for slaughter is not debatable. But Singer's argument comes close to the ethical pathos of abolitionists arguing for the better treatment, even emancipation, of slaves, granting freed slaves—as Frederick Douglass knew—some utility, even understanding, but never respect, not the privilege of possessing their own thought or speaking to their own people.

Singer counters reasonableness against degrees of incapacity— capable of more or less reason—as a necessary bulwark against cruelty. What, then, do these rights so urgently invoked look like, and legally, how would they be constituted? In arguing against Singer, Hearne used to talk about his indifference to consciousness, memory, and judgment—the personal identity—of animals. As she never tired of saying, humanitarian claims reduced dogs to objects of charity, or worse, to servile recipients of their masters' beneficence. Easy certainty undermines what matters most in the mutuality of adaptation between humans and dogs.

The greatest dog I ever had was the worst dog, or so I thought at the beginning. Mehdi hated and feared men, especially arrogant, tall ones. He bit them. He attacked a rather macho dog trainer one day in the backyard of my house in Tucson. I found him wandering around Oak Creek Canyon in Sedona, Arizona. He looked like a deer. Abandoned, he had fleas in his ears and ate only leaves and insects. I tried to teach him to eat meat or sit for dog biscuits, but he always preferred lettuce and anything green. He was an American Staffordshire terrier. Mehdi was also a good judge of character. He went for the balls of particularly pompous men. When I injured my back not long after I found him, he became more aggressive. He went after a colleague who came to visit me. Another colleague, and, yes, another male who was well meaning and caring, explained that sometimes euthanasia is the only answer. After all, he explained, he and his former wife had a dog that ate shoes. They could not get him to stop. So they killed him. For this professor there was no such thing as training. Only coaxing was allowed. Discipline held no appeal for him. It was too cruel.

Vicki lay dying in a hospice in Connecticut. After she died, I drove from Tucson, my home of ten years, to the East Coast. I decided to search for Red River, the site of John Wayne's film of cows and honor. Once past Fort Stockton, Bakersfield, and Ozona, I realized I had not found it. On the way to San Antonio, I stopped for the night. Getting out of the car with my dogs, I knew that this first night outside Tucson marked the end of a kind of peace, the sun and sky that left humans in awe of things not often remarked on or known: the precise grasp of a Harris's hawk; the summer dance of the tarantulas; the wolf spider pulsing in the corner of a room; the wail of the Colorado River toads after August monsoons; footprints left in the dirt by the nighttime wandering of the javelina; long-backed lizards pressed against the windows; and coyotes searching for kill as bulldozers devoured the Sonoran Desert.

Let the elegy begin. The turn to things lost, the end of much that I loved. In the humid summer of Philadelphia, I understood the meaning of that thing I saw in Sonora, outside of San Antonio. After feeding Dogie, Mehdi, and Jesse, I went out to the car to get my bags. I saw something stuck to the front grill of my car. A bird on the grill. In the night wind, the thing that once had been a sparrow must have flown toward the headlights. Trying to get it off, using a pencil and then a large comb, I saw that its guts were stuck, wrapped into the steel. Stuck by its guts. A curse, I thought. The next day, as I drove through sun into heavy rain, I prayed that it would fall to the ground. Instead, the sparrow held on all the way to Philadelphia. Once there, when I parked the car across the street from my new house, the bird finally dropped off. Dried out in the heat, it fell to the ground, hollowed out and folded like a dead leaf.

The life it asks of us is a dog's life.
JAMES MERRILL, "THE VICTOR DOG"

BECAUSE YOU LOOK AROUND and find them looking at you. Then you become yourself to yourself. You exist. Your home has meaning. But that is not exactly it. It is not about me, but about flesh shot through with spirit, the dogs so adamantly in their bodies that they become mind. It is about the thought of dogs.

Dogie, the old Rottweiler, sits downstairs in the only comfortable chair in the house. Mehdi and Jesse, accustomed to being walked every morning, sit on either side of my chair as I try to write. This is their daily ritual. They wait for me to put on their leashes. They run downstairs and sit together at the door. Sometimes Jesse begins to tremble and refuses to go out while Mehdi, already out on the stoop, continues to wait. I usually end up removing Jesse's choke collar and give up, shutting the door in her face. Then Mehdi and I take our walk to the dog park on the banks of the Schuylkill, and I get lost in the life of dogs.

I know there is a connection between my life alone with the dogs and the life of the spirit that I hold tight within me. Both the demands of the dogs and the belief in the spirit separate me from the world of summer: the possibilities of going for a swim, out to lunch, or taking the train to New York to see friends. Which came first? Was I saddled with dogs, taking the obligation to care for them as the only serious task; and only then, having deprived myself of the things I once loved in order to be with them, did I turn to Saint Paul? Or had I already understood the renunciation necessary to receive Christ in me, and then the dogs arrived, all three of them, and I took them to be the form of my test of faith?

I was ready for Christ but remained with a house of dogs. But that sequence might not be right. Here I sit in the upper room, on the third floor of a row house in Center City, Philadelphia, with three dogs. They could be the things that hold me captive and so quiet that I can think about Saint Paul answering for the body and blood of the Lord. In this life of digression where I hold

myself in a hiatus from the kinds of summer that I once enjoyed, the dogs have become my only reality. Strung out between two inconceivables: the thought of my dogs and the life of the spirit.

I lived in a world of dogs. They carried such beauty into my daily life that I wince recalling my days with them. Each day was marked by the thoughts of dogs, their barks, their whines, their eating and pissing, their love. I lost a lot when I left the desert of the Tucson Mountains. But I had my dogs. They brought with them all that I had lost.

They are all dead now. Dogie died at eleven. At ten, Jesse was hit by a car. Mehdi died in his sleep at fifteen and is buried in my backyard in Nashville. I named him "Mehdi," Arabic for "guide" or "messenger." He had four blond eyebrows like the Zoroastrian dog of the beyond. But I always translated "Mehdi" as "messiah" and called him "Mehdi dog," the dog that delivered me from sorrow.

I am still lost in the life of dogs. Everything I know of the spirit I learned from them. Straddling the divide between heaven and earth, dogs were always my test of faith. They hold me captive in their love. Their ghosts are with me still.

Dogie died under strange circumstances. He had spent only two years in Philadelphia when something happened while he was boarding at Red Bank Veterinary Hospital in New Jersey. At Red Bank, dogs became patients. Just a year before that, while I was in Princeton on a fellowship, Dogie had undergone surgery for spindle cell sarcoma. He recovered. His image from that time of healing was preserved on page 7 in the Red Bank brochure. He was lying on a very low table, his body stretched out, very relaxed, his face turned in trust, gazing up at the doctor.

Gentle and gracious Dogie. Now eleven years old, he often coughed at night, breathed heavily, and sometimes needed to slow his pace as he regained his balance. Garnering his strength to preserve our relation, he held the poise between strength and frailty. Something happened to Dogie that night at Red Bank. In an early-morning call, the veterinarian tried to explain: "The old dog had trouble breathing, so we did what we could to help him." When I arrived at the hospital, they told me that Dogie was waiting in a room they had set aside for me. Once alone with him, I spoke his favorite words: "Let's go for a walk." "Want to go home?" He seemed broken. His gums had lost their color. The blood was out of them, the flesh pulled up into his teeth. He had trouble standing. I sat next to him on the floor. Then Dogie lay down and put his beautiful and massive head on my right knee. His form was changed, as if crushed by some heavy metal. I bent over him. The doctor told me that they tried to tap his chest for fluid and discontinued it when they drew blood. I bent over Dogie. He had changed utterly from the dog that had run with me by the river just two days earlier.

I decided to put him to sleep. After the lethal injection, his eyes would not close. "I can't close his eyes. They're still half open," I said to the doctor who euthanized him. "Often dogs' eyes don't close." The door opened, and the tech who had seen him six hours earlier screamed. "Dogie, what happened to Dogie? He was fine last night. Why is he dead? Who killed him?" I knew I had done wrong. A mistaken idea about mercy, an unthinking response to some cliché about "putting him out of his misery." Had I killed a sedated dog? Was there some miscommunication between doctors? A radiance remembered haunted me.

Had I given him a chance, I wondered, would he have lived? Killing him as quickly as I did was a sign not of strength but of stupidity. Consider the particulars of my choice, the scene of surrender. The doctor advised me not to let him suffer. "He's an  old dog anyway." "He's lived a good life." But who has the right to define suffering? Instead of listening to these piecemeal offerings of dubious feeling, I should have taken him from that hospital, helped him to breathe again, to gain life from the stresses and glories of what he loved most. Early the next morning, he would have stood up. Never give up what you love. Behold, Dogie, gentle Dogie. Stand up and unfold yourself. "Let's go for a walk," I spoke his favorite words a little too loudly. "Want to go home?"

A month after his death, after numerous requests for the records of his last days, and varied and conflicting stories, the woman in charge of cremation called: "I don't know how to tell you this. It's never happened here before. We've lost Dogie's cremains. We've looked everywhere." I remained silent. I heard her say something about sending me a check to reimburse me. Unlike the records, promised but evidently never sent, this time a check arrived by Federal Express the next day. A check for the cost of cremation at Pleasant Grove Pet Cemetery and a form with an *X* in the box that marked "refund from Red Bank Veterinary Hospital." It reminded me of the dubious meaning of redemption: to buy back or recover, a transaction that trades in the merging of high and low. Death for human beings who kill, but if the object of the kill is an animal, then the human "shall make restitution for it," as the Lord tells Moses in Leviticus.

The Gospel according to Matthew tells an animal story that has not received much attention. It is repeated with some changes in Mark. A parable it is not, for it sets dogs in a precise relation to salvation in a way that is quite accountable, and not altogether unimaginable. Several chapters before this story, however, we read the passage often recalled for containing the "don't cast your pearls before swine" admonition. The entirety of that warning reads: "Do not give what is holy to dogs; and do not throw your pearls before swine, or they will trample them under foot and turn and maul you" (7:6). Do we ever hear now, "Hey, don't give what's holy to dogs"? And yet dogs are there and probably are the referent of "they," who will "turn" and "maul." Having domesticated dogs, we cannot reckon them as swine.

Here, then, is Matthew's story of faith and service. A Canaanite woman from the district of Tyre and Sidon, in other words, a gentile, shouts, "Have mercy on me, Lord, Son of David: my daughter is tormented by a demon" (15:22). As often when he is recognized, Jesus refuses to recognize the source of recognition. The Canaanite comes and kneels at his feet. "Lord, help me." Instead of immediately answering her plea, he responds, "It is not fair to take the children's food and throw it to the dogs." Thus, with the call of substitution and justice, their exchange begins. "Yes, Lord, yet even the dogs eat the crumbs that fall from their master's table." (In Mark, the dogs are positioned explicitly "under the table.") We are faced with the delicacy of subordination, both that of the woman and that of her dogs. Jesus answers her. "Woman, great is your faith! Let it be done for you as you wish" (15:21–28). Her daughter is healed and no longer possessed. Not so figurative as throwing pearls before swine, or as dramatic as Christ casting out Legion's demons into the Gadarene swine, but exacting and particular, simply throwing children's food before dogs. How has her answer proved her faith? According to Matthew Henry's *Commentary on the Whole Bible* (1708–1710), those whom Christ means most to honor, he first humbles. The gentiles, unlike the chosen, the children of Israel, come forth as unworthy as dogs. But so satiated are these privileged children that they throw away both meat and sweetness, leaving the refuse as crumbs for those ready to receive.

The transactions that redefine power in Matthew's story of miraculous cure substitute an unruly Pauline materiality for the pressure of punishment in Jewish law. And dogs anchor us anew in a place we can inhabit, where memory of day, night, love, and hate, once pondered, soars in righteousness as real as light, the final grace of unarguable justice. This story gives meaning to habitation, to what it means to abide in and with others, whether they assume the shape of animals or humans. No longer do we hear about death; now we hear of hunger and satiation. Not about sanctification but about redemption. Jesus distinguishes between "whatever goes into the mouth" and "what comes out of the mouth." For what goes into the mouth ends up in the muck, but what comes out has its origins in the heart and is thus all that can really defile: "evil intentions, murder, adultery, fornication, theft, false witness, slander" (15:19).

Are dogs really the least of all God's mercies? Here, perhaps for the only time in the Hebrew Bible or the New Testament, dogs have something to do with salvation. As the most common thing, at the opposite end of holiness, they wait. They are the last to get the crumbs. And in that waiting, their still presence leads the way, thus becoming the medium for a new kind of salvation. In a world where dogs and women and the poor and diseased together receive both what is thrown away and what is treasured, death no longer pollutes.

After Dogie died, I began to wonder about the thought of dogs and the life of the spirit. Surely, I thought, in this call of bodies rapt in and riddled through with spirit, animals would walk differently on the earth. Surpassing the surrender of the goat to Azazel, Jesus's work on the cross—in breaking the power of sin, in atoning for us all by his blood—must mean that death would be different, even for dogs. "But someone will ask: How are the dead raised? With what kind of body do they come?" (1 Cor. 15:35).

Spirits rise up as the dogs yawn, crack their joints, and stretch. Dogs counsel us to learn that no thing, no one ever gives up the ghost, even when flesh and bone are consumed. "Handle me and see for a spirit hath not flesh and bones" (Luke 24:39), translated in the Oxford New Revised Standard Edition more exactly, if more distressingly, as: "Touch me and see; for a ghost does not have flesh and bone." To be resurrected from dry bones and putrid flesh into the spirit of God, before God, when the world is no more. "How are the dead raised?" "Stand up and unfold yourself." Will the body be as it was in life, rising up without a leg, as a fetus, or with the neck marked by the hangman's noose?

I had a dream of Dogie, who returned to me in the night as an ancestor spirit, speaking to me in a dream, as do the gods in Haiti. He ran through green fields, as if through Elysium, though actually he romped in Sussex Park, across the street from my old house, the one I loved. We were all there, my parents, my vet from Tucson, and I. He looked beautiful. We acknowledged his presence with the words, "He's all right. He's all right." Dogie in the grass. Dogie dreaming himself home. He let me know that even though I did not have his ashes, I had him still.

As time passed, my other two dogs, Mehdi and Jesse, brought Dogie back into my presence. Now they are dead. But let me remember them through the way they called Dogie to mind.

At night, not long after his death, they become Dogie. He enters their bodies. They look at me in peace. He stands up again, not just once and not as he died, but often, in the bodies of his companions. An intimacy of spirit embodied in the flesh. This possession occurs first late one night on the third floor in the Philadelphia house, where Dogie liked to sleep. Jesse lies on her bed, stretched out, her features turning sharp, her little eyes growing larger, working their way into her older brother's melancholy stare. Mehdi, who adored Dogie, comes before me that same night, brings his lineaments into conformation with Dogie's thick but radiant disarray:

one back leg stretched out very long, as he curled up on his side. Then he takes yet another position, as he breathes out the sigh of an old dog. Front legs loosely encircle the back legs, which are straight, stiff, and parallel, pulled up under the chest. Mehdi and I lie down together on the sofa and bring Dogie back from sleep. I rub Mehdi's nose, and then, to my shock, he makes the churlish, clucking sound—something like a loud lick flexed into a gulp, tongue curled, eyes closed—that Dogie used to take me deeply to heart.

These dogs, often distant from Dogie during his life, become tender and close in his passing. Redemption is sure. The bargain has been made. Mehdi performs the logic of exchange in a ritual of memory and resurrection of times and places past that seemed irreplaceable. I am in the kitchen on one of the humid nights in Philadelphia. It is midnight. Mehdi sits down in front of me, soberly stares, and brings Dogie back, as he was in Tucson seven years earlier. Dogie takes up a position in space and time, bringing me back to a relation I had thought as dead as dust. Mehdi does the unparalleled "up Simba" on the patio in the desert, a trick he never saw, done before he was born. The position required that Dogie sit with his back haunches on the floor, a normal sit. Then, at the summons "up Simba," the body pulled up miraculously, and Dogie reared upright, vertical, as if standing still, paws up like those of a lion in a circus.

In a flush of heat and wonder, everything comes back to me. Mehdi fills out, enhanced by Dogie's body in its most complete and disciplined form. No waiting for the world to wear away, the moon to turn red, the whore of Babylon to ride forth. Instead, right here, right now, Mehdi grows into Dogie and hears my voice. And I watch, in wonder, again, knowing that dogs never forget and never let go. Immersed in flesh, Mehdi takes on Dogie's thought as his own. As if listening for the pulse of the mind in him that is nothing other than Dogie's consciousness, both dogs become one and call on me to know belief as real as a fist to the stomach, as palpable as an embrace.

chapter two

back talking like i did

I LEFT THE SOUTH AT SIXTEEN. I never intended to return. Now I can't leave.

It is just like I remembered it. And nine years later I am still here, longer than I have stayed anywhere except Atlanta, where I was born and raised. I came here because my mother was dying. I left the Northeast to live again in the heat with too much green, moths dying on lightbulbs, and neighbors walking up and down the street, too briskly, as if their lives depended on it.

There are also the white men tall and proud and their eyes so bold and fearless. But I am not scared anymore like I was. Because I walk with Stella, my American Staffordshire who is always recognized as a pit bull terrier, I can go down the street and look straight into their eyes when they stare at me from their trucks. Their smiles make me feel good. Their gaze takes me to a place of comfort that I don't understand. They give me a respite from the meanness, the gossip, and the sense I get that I don't belong, that I am not right in my skin.

What that something is I do not know. But I have a hunch that it has a lot to do with terror. I grew up when big white men with guns and dogs were patrolling the streets and talking on the television news. My parents kept me close in their sights. I hated their control. I did not belong in that house. They drank. They partied. They traveled. They brought back antiques. But no matter how much money they spent, they never seemed to have any fun. They listened to Frank Sinatra, told bawdy jokes, and yelled at me. My mother did not like me. She told me I looked "like a Ubangi" and added, "I don't know where you came from looking like you do with that ugly face of yours."

I had nowhere to go. I was as afraid of my mother's scorn as I was of the violence of the white men who kicked and spat at demonstrators two blocks from my father's store. But I was not part of that either. I belonged nowhere. Everything happened as if through a long, dark tunnel. I crouched way in the back of it and looked out. I could not get close to the scary white men or the brave black students or the two people who called themselves my mother and father who showed me off to their friends. Trussed and pert like a pig, I was made ready for viewing, but they wanted nothing to do with me as soon as we got home.

I was saved by Lucille, the black woman from Jamaica who came into my life when I was two years old. She told me that when she sat down on the sofa for her interview, I jumped up in her lap and would not move. "Nobody could pry you from me," she said. Without her I never would have known eyes that did not hate or harden at the sight of me. She did not like dogs or men. Took Johnny the Pekingese out back and chained him to the garage and locked the albino poodle with freckles that my mother named Pepe (after *Pépé le Moko*) in the bathroom. But all that didn't matter to me. She told me stories about ghosts who landed in white skin on the window ledge, taught me how to tell one kind of cricket from another, showed me where in the creek I could find the biggest cottonmouth water moccasins, and gave me long lectures about men, mostly about how to live much better without them.

I was thirteen in 1963 when Martin Luther King Jr. wrote his Letter from Birmingham Jail, when the four girls died in the Sixteenth Street Baptist Church bombing there, when Kennedy was assassinated in Dallas and Ngo Dinh Diem in Saigon. Malcolm X suffered Elijah Muhammad's discipline of public silence after he described Kennedy's murder as a case of "the chickens coming home to roost." In Atlanta, "the city too busy to hate," Lester Maddox took up the Confederate flag, iron skillets, and ax handles at his Pickrick Restaurant to block "colored folk" from entry. My father's friend Charlie Leb (born Lebedin) dragged the Reverend Ashton Jones by his feet across the floor and out the door of his restaurant on 66 Luckie Street. Then, with the promise of free deli lunches, Leb encouraged white crackers to spit on and beat up young protesters from Morehouse and Spelman Colleges.

But I found ways out of the South. I saw a photo of the gorgeous legs of Christine Keeler in the backseat of a limo. God, she was pretty. I didn't think much about sex then, but I figured there must be some connection between long white legs, a skirt hiked up high above the knees, and a man named Profumo who got what he deserved. I listened to the song "Oxford Town" on Bob Dylan's second album, *The Freewheelin' Bob Dylan*, and memorized every line of Nancy Wilson's "Bewitched, Bothered and Bewildered" on *Yesterday's Love Songs/Today's Blues*. I could stay in the house, locked up in my room, and think about hate and love.

Hate was in the eyes of the white men who were tall and proud. Hate caused fires to start, glass to break, guns to kill, clubs to hit, dogs to chase and bite. The dogs were big. They were German shepherds, not the blue tick or red bone hounds used to scent out black slaves and then prisoners. Through it all I saw the eyes of the white men. Not just the eyes. Their mouths were smiling. They grinned as they beat up people kneeling in prayer. They smirked as they circled around reporters whose cameras they smashed.

Now, fifty years later, when I see white men looking at my dog and me, I quicken in sight of their smiles. Are they grinning because they like the breed? Inviting me to bond with them in having a game dog, a loyal dog that knows no fear and never gives up? Or is it that same old lethal grin, telling me with their eyes and in the twist of their lips that I might be walking now but they could hobble or cripple me anytime they wanted?

My parents must have had some kind of fear too, because they made it clear that I could never go out by myself. When I was old enough to drive they told me where not to go, when not to talk. I learned that driving south of Atlanta, to Barnesville on the way to Florida, was to be on the lookout for pickup trucks, to lock the doors and roll up the windows at red lights, to be sure that I had enough gas to get through small towns. But driving north up to Helen, Georgia, in the mountains right at the head of the Appalachian Trail, I would be safer. I could stop at gas stations. I never got close to one of these white men. But I always thought of them as real because they became the touchstone for what I could not do, where I could not go, what I could never be. Closer to reality than anything I knew, they looked natural, strong and sure, and cruel. Worried and anxious, alternately prudent and reckless, my parents tried too hard to live well and impress lavishly. I never trusted them. Their cruelty to me always came packaged like care.

I lived strung out between two extremes. The look of my father, hurt by my mother's infidelity, but too proud to let it show. A man of books who worried constantly and regretted everything he had not done or would not do. Then there was the look of the men that I could never get near, who were always up high in a truck or standing strong on a porch. The white men who would not take shit from anyone, who knew what they liked, and knew who did not deserve to live. Not only could they kill. They toyed with, tortured, and trashed.

Except for Lucille, women never figured in my life except as examples of what I never wanted to be. These women talked on the phone all day, shopped, got manicures, flirted, and seemed wildly beautiful to me though deeply unlikeable, like the stamens of a magnolia gone to rot. How could I like women who lived in the shadow of men? So I decided early on not to wear makeup, not to entice. I enjoyed walking barefoot, playing with frogs, and tearing the heads off dolls. If I ever had to put on a dress—a prom gown or something—I felt I was in drag. Obsessed with the Church and Christ on the cross, I decided to become a nun. Instead, I became a professor.

I studied. I wrote books. I did all the things my mother warned me not to do: talked about serious things, got involved in political discussions. Just like "a librarian," she used to taunt. "A dried up prune," she laughed. "You'll be left holding the bag." Sometimes she added words that seemed to me the worst curse of all: "You'll end up behind the ape ball." It wasn't until decades later, not until a few years ago, that I learned that she was saying "behind the eight ball," the black ball in pool that meant absolute loss, not something meant only for apes.

Now I'm back where it all began, with the lightning bugs, the extra large mosquitoes that Lucille called "gabber nipples," the road kill, the possums in the night, the stray dogs, the crickets chirping, and the tall white men. My mother is back, too. After she died, all her things arrived here in my house: the old Italian paintings, the jewelry, the silver, the hundreds upon hundreds of photos that my father took of her in every pose all over the world. She is here where she wants to be, going through her things and laughing at me while she pleads with me to be close, to get down with her on the bed and talk through the night, dropping hints to me about Haiti, about the man she loved who was not my father. I learned right after she died that the house I bought here in Nashville is two streets away from where she and my father lived just after their marriage. Who knows what happened when a young girl of seventeen left New York with a man who was twenty years older, when a spirited beauty found herself with the dour son of a rabbi? They never told me about living in Nashville, and after she died I found only one photo of them here. They sat at a table with other couples at a restaurant where an appliance store now stands. My mother had a white camellia in her long, dark hair.

No matter how fast it grows, Nashville is small, "close as a possum's crotch," as a friend put it. Everyone knows where everyone else belongs, where everyone came from, and no one seems to mind. Life appears easy and relaxed. There are more spas, beauty salons, and aestheticians than I have seen anywhere else. Plastic surgery, laser treatments, fillers, peels, Botox, and lots of blond hair bleached through with highlights. White skin like parchment, drawn tight and so thin that the blue veins show through. These women outdo anything I ever saw growing up in Atlanta. Body hair is not to be trusted. Maybe this is also the rage in other places. I can't be sure. But here white men and women take every last bit of pubic hair right off. Skin must be smooth as glass.

"Oh Lord," I used to be told, "your hair is so thick." And there I sat trying to get the look my mother had always wanted. Now that she is around all the time, I guess I reckoned it was time to get it nice and straight. So there I remained, hours on end, enduring heat from the blow dryer and the pull of a flat iron, only to see in the mirror a person who had become the woman she never wanted to be. Well, not exactly. I looked more like a corpse with someone else's hair. I mean that I was dead just like my mother, living her life and copying half-heartedly a kind of elegance that always sat uneasily on me. So I cut off all my hair, clean off.

I live a life that comes out sounding like some kind of a joke. I could never tell the difference between life and death anyway, with all the ghosts Lucille called out at night: ghosts of little girls bit by spiders, husbands whose legs were lost in cotton mills or torn off by scythes in the field, white women whom lust had worn down like the heels of shoes. So whether I'm dead or alive, me or my mother, I never knew. Until now, with the hair cut clean off and "tight and curly" as Lucille used to say, I know who I am and who I always wanted to be.

I am a woman who grew up in terror. Not Lucille's ghosts. I always thought of them when I read about Yeats's "White woman that passion has worn."[1] But those white men. They are with me still. I am not afraid anymore to stop at the gas stations because of the men who might look at me as if they wanted to kill me. I am now looking for those men. They are defining the work that I choose to do. I remember their barely suppressed laughs, scaring, as I used to say, the "living daylights out of me." I hanker after that raw, southern hate.

They still do not like me. I know it. Their friendliness, like my respect, puts us all at the edge of what is permissible. We are all faking it. Terror is always like that. It skirts the real. It looks to the past. And the dialogue carries the old scorn in its pauses. I like it. I get to fake politeness and live again the fright. I live again an intensity that comes only with the risk and the knowledge that I am at last where my parents never wanted me to be.

It is all so complicated. And I am always so dishonest.

ONE NIGHT NOT LONG after a quick marriage in Nashville, I left my husband's bed. I carried my pillows, told my dogs I was going, and moved down the hall into the room with the daybed. It was hot, though the air-conditioning was on. That's how summer is in Nashville. With the temperature set at seventy-one degrees in the house, when it is over twenty degrees hotter outside at midnight, no cool air remains upstairs. Stella and Mehdi, the dogs, waited while I pulled back the winter quilt and spread it out again to form a soft base for us on the hard mattress. When I crawled in under the sheet, they came up beside me.

I used to sleep with my dogs every night, before my husband forbade their presence. So I remembered the old days with my dogs, how well they got along and how happily I used to sleep with them. I looked at photos of the dogs, photos in the Tucson desert and in the trinity house in Philadelphia. Dogie, Jesse, and Mehdi. Mehdi was the last of the Tucson dogs. Dogie, who died the unseemly death in Red Bank, was the first casualty of my mother's illness and my aunt's aggression. But that's another story.

In trying to make sense of my life, I think about my dogs and their deaths. When I began dating my husband, Jesse ran away. I wonder now whether this was her warning to me. Dogs sense change. They know the irretrievable before bad things come to pass. They can sense the future but they also remember everything—how I breathe, when I smile. I never saw Jesse again after her escape. After my weeklong search for her, a neighbor told me that she heard about a dog that was hit by a car, left to die on the road, unclaimed. Metro Animal Control took the body away and dumped it in an incinerator.

THE SUN COMES THROUGH MY WINDOW. I hear a lick and turn around. It is Stella I see. She came from a kennel in Pennsylvania that raised American Staffordshire terriers and Arabians. The purebred daughter of champions, she is the only one of my dogs that I did not rescue. She is the saving remnant, the one who still lives after Mehdi died. She is stout, muscular, and black. Though she has none of his grace or constancy, she bears some of his traits. Diligently copied during his life, they became more pronounced after his death: the vehement lick and the stretching of her legs as if more fully to sense her breath.

Stella looks like an "Eli Dog," named for Floyd Boudreaux's line going all the way back to when dog fighting was legal and his dogs were known to be the best, with the biggest hearts and unstoppable energy. Stella's loyalty is so intense that I meet her eyes with won-

der. People call her a pit bull, but she is stouter and closer to the ground with shorter legs. Watching her, I know now what it means to be a dog that will jump to the top of a fence, run back and forth along it for what seems like eternity, every sense and muscle taut with desire, just because there is the neighbor's dog, a Scottish terrier named Muffin, on the other side.

This book began with a marriage, a bond that turned me into something not exactly human. Referred to repeatedly as a "wife," I began to feel more like a dog. I earned a right to know the meaning of domination, to know what it meant to live by command, in fear but also with great attentiveness. I looked at my dogs and I knew that in their eyes, in the form of their knowledge, so bodily, I could feel something good and positive. That was the only divinity or wonder left in my life.

I lived on the knife-edge of cruelty. I learned what it meant to be cared for and how threatening that solicitude could be. I also understood what were for me the perils of reason, the ways that the call for the sensible or the decent could be forms of coercion that were difficult to fight against. Closeness, or a rightness in standing next to or close to my dogs, became a way of thinking through the terror and sentimentality of this, our twenty-first century. Where is there to go except into the eyes of dogs?

One night Stella jumped on our bed. It was 9:45. My husband pulled her by the scruff of her neck, dragged her off the bed onto the floor, and yelled, "Stay." He wanted to punish her for what she had done. She walked off. He dragged her back. She ran out of the room. Then he left, and we were free. Stella and I went walking in the rain. We ran into the house, I toweled her dry, and then she jumped, at last. Onto the sofa! All of a sudden I heard the crickets rubbing their legs, so I ran upstairs and there she was. She had come there before me. I shouted, "It's okay, dog. No more fear, no more punishment!"

So it was morning in Nashville, very cold, very crisp and star-tling. But my husband was yelling at my dog. She liked to sit on his pillow where he put his head and pee on his Oriental rug. But when I was home and he was gone, she behaved. Mice, dogs, and possum. I thought about Wallace Stevens's "No Possum, No Sop, No Taters": "The field is frozen. The leaves are dry / Bad is final in this light."[2]

Late one night in autumn, my husband took me into the kitchen. There was a small mouse on the counter, crushed and covered in blood but alive. My husband explained that he bought traps as soon as he saw a mouse. This mouse was in the trap but not dead. I asked him what he did in the past if a trap had not killed a mouse. He told me that he killed it. I pressed him to tell me how. "Beat it to death," he said. "With what?" I asked. "With a shoe," he answered.

Blood. Beating. How often in the past year have I heard, sometimes in jest, "I'm going to beat her." I remember now how he hit her nose, chased her around the house. The little dog Stella, the puppy he sometimes cooed over. Violence that I could not remember knowing, except later as I recalled when my father—good Edmund, gentle Edmund, angelic Edmund—chased me out of the den and into the kitchen and out of the house with his belt in his hand. He was going to "strap" me, he screamed.

My husband got rid of the mouse. He put out other traps. But the mice outsmarted him. Ate the peanut butter under the metal lever but escaped the crush of it. Their shit was everywhere. I convinced my husband to stop leaving the traps. Slowly but surely the mice stopped coming, the shit stopped dropping. But he looked every morning for signs of them. Sometimes he found one piece of shit and let me know that they were still here.

I stopped eating meat or fish. I could no longer stand the sight of cooked flesh. I began to identify with animals, my dogs especially. I called out to them, sometimes while I worked at the computer, "Hello, mammals!" We were in it together. We were the primitives, the ones who needed to be corrected and controlled. It was disconcerting to me that Stella—the American Staffordshire who experienced most fully the wrath of my husband, screaming and throwing himself at her in a rage—loved him the most. If he deigned to look at her, bend down, and pet her, that tail wagged in a fury. She lay there as if she had waited all her life for his touch.

Stella learned to be ornery. Confused by the differences between my husband and me, the demonic ambiguity of the household, she could be fierce. In the last year of Mehdi's life, she attacked him twice. Perhaps she wanted to take his light, the thought in his eyes, the grace of his limbs. She bit him twice, first on the right ear, then on the left. The second time was worse than the first, ripping the ear, tearing off the soft skin that I liked to nuzzle. It happened once when she wanted to be the first on the stairs to go up to bed and the next time when she sensed that I was going to give him a bone before her. But he loved her. No wound could stop that.

Mehdi died in his sleep when he was fifteen years old. Maybe the anesthesia for his stitches, a nighttime surgery for each ear Stella tore, wore him out. He had already lived through so much, accommodated himself to so much when Stella entered his life. Both dogs slept in their beds in my study. They enjoyed switching beds or sleeping together. But sometimes Stella did not want to let him up the stairs. Standing at the top on the landing, she stared him down, and he knew not to come up. He stood there stock still looking at her. I told Stella to lie down. Then Mehdi came up to join her, and all was calm.

Mehdi loved Stella. His lust was always surprising. The night before he died, he humped her. Her energy and gusto excited him. Whenever she played hard and long, going after a ball or tree-ing a squirrel, he took her hind legs in his front legs; and pulling them into his chest and under him, he began to hump. She became very still, not exactly resigned but meditative in a rare moment of acquiescence.

they killed my dog

IN HAITI, FOLKS BELIEVE that when you take someone's picture you steal their soul. Maybe that is what happened to my mother and me.

Where was the injury? When did everything change? Hundreds, no, thousands of photos: my father overdid everything. How many times must a door be checked before you are sure that it is locked?

Looking through pages and pages of contact sheets of my mother posing for my father, I find many of me: never as glamorous, but just as numerous. I was young. My father followed me everywhere with his camera. That I did not remember. But now I see me in a corner, on the bed, on a sofa, sometimes in a slip, sometimes dressed. I am not posing. I am running away. Trying to hide.

I look at one of the photos on the contact sheet. A dog tag around my neck and wearing a slip, I look over at the camera but not as if I see anything. I do not. I seem to be frozen in terror; standing on the bed, I am as close to the wall as I can get. Not crouching or cowering but stiff and straight as if I thought I could just fade away. I can go into the wall, as long as I concentrate on being still.

They killed my dog.

Dogs. The last real thing. It all began with the corpse of a dog. The rot of love and the stink of disposal.

I remembered the photo of Lucille and me with Johnny the Pekingese. I had seen it many times. A little snapshot, not at all like the formal enlargements my father made. Out in the backyard, down in the dirt next to the dog, I squatted with my legs open and my panties showing. Lucille bent down behind us, as if to frame us in her arms. She used to chain Johnny outside by the garage. One day my mother brought home a white poodle with pink skin, freckles, and squinting eyes. "Like a china dog," she used to say. "Not a real poodle." I remembered taking him into the bathroom on his birthday and making a cake for him out of towels.

Dogie was my own first dog, who barked when he saw me at the Humane Society in Tucson. A Rottweiler, I named him for my father's favorite song, which my father tried to remember right before he died: "Git along little dogies, git along." I had no idea at the time that "dogies" were "dough-guts" or orphaned calves. Abandoned by their mothers, they were identified by their bellies, which seemed to be nothing more than a batch of sourdough carried in a sack. Nor did I know then that the song was about the last roundup, about dying: "I'm headin' for the last roundup / Gonna saddle Old Paint for the last time and ride." Jesse the black Labrador and Mehdi the Am Staff followed Dogie's arrival. These dogs changed my life. I wondered how I had lived all those years in New York without dogs, without their breath on my face and their warmth in my bed.

Nothing mattered to me like these dogs. No man could be as close, no eyes as vivid, no flesh as necessary. On the ground with them, I would bend close into one dog face, so close that I could make my tooth clink against a tooth, my hand on the paw, pulling it out straight, feeling the pulse in my fingers. They were my life. The dogs. Something deep and vital that could never be taken away from me came with them into my home or pressed close to me in the bed. I made up songs for them. "Dogie dog, Dogie dog, riding through the glen, with his band of men, with his band of men." Never before had I known anything incorruptible, so strong and blooded. I sometimes wondered why they meant more to me than anything I had ever known before and why their deaths were to be remembered with all the stillness of worship, with an immensity of regret I never could muster for any human, not my parents, not for anyone I ever knew.

I found out later why dogs became the ruling passion of my life. Out of the piles of photos, I found one contact sheet of a dog and me, a dog I had never seen before. I had no memories about this dog. But now, here he is right before me. In the photos, he sits close to me. Very conscious of my presence, he looks up at me with what I see now as tenderness. Tan and white, he is a hound, most certainly, a tree walker coonhound, I think. As far from the little Pekingese or albino poodle as could be. The photos must have been taken when I was three or four, out in the back of the house on Briarcliff Road. The house with the linoleum floors in the kitchen, the stone stairs with wooden handrails out back, the steep driveway where the Buick Roadmaster rolled down backward one morning when my mother forgot to put on the brake. There in the kitchen my mother sometimes stood at the stove, with light coming into the window and setting her face aglow.

He was my dog. He had to be. So it was with him out there in the yard that I first held on to a dog leg, bent down with my face next to a dog face. I looked into his eyes with a radiance that appears in no other photo of me, anywhere, at any place. He looks at me. We are posing together. In one shot I pull on his leg, my hand around his ankle. In another, I lie down next to him on the grass, with my head on his flank, and then in the next one, I press my face close and clench my teeth tight just like he does.

Something terrible must have happened, so bad that I never knew about this dog, the dog that was mine. What could have been done to me, I always wondered, to make me hate my parents, to want to get away from them always, even at five when we moved to Plymouth Road and I packed a bag and hid it under the bed, longing to escape. Dead dog. Gone dog. Out of my mind until now.

So it wasn't the usual abuse, back then in Atlanta, just a father who cornered me with his camera when he wasn't chasing me out the back door with his belt; a mother who told me to leave her alone and act nicely for company; and a dog that I loved so much that he had to die. Just like my two white leghorn chickens killed by the yardman when I was ten so that they could be frozen and eaten. They were mine, too. I raised them from chicks and cared for them out back. I remember them. I saw the hatchet and watched Thomas chase them down. They danced in the sunlight without their heads. The last time I saw Thomas, we sat together in the house in Atlanta. He remembered the chicken blood in the rain. "You cried all day long. You caught hell," Thomas said, "for looking out the wrong side of your eye."

In looking at these photos, I see that they are the only ones that show me with eyes that see and a face that expresses something like amazement or joy in proximity to the dog that I never remembered. I look alive. Oh that word means that the head is attached to the neck in a way that does not look brittle like the cockeyed twist of my head when I posed before my father's camera.

This one sheet of photos with the dog that was mine—my mother never would have sat down on the ground with a dog that could not be held—shows me in a way I never knew as myself in childhood. No dark circles around the eyes, gazing out with fear and hesitation, as if I had been caught crying. No weakness. Instead, I stand with my mouth open in relief, squat with my eyes intense with concentration as I pull hardily at the dog leg with a dog face looking at me. I bow down before the dog that looks away at that moment. But he knows I am there. Only with him beside me can I look into the camera not like a broken doll but whole in myself, my pleasure giving an effect of wildness, almost of rapid water, contained only by the force of my love. The containment comes across in these photos in softness that I never saw again—except with dogs. We are together. Cognizant of my every move, the dog waits, all knowing, waits for the next touch, the next embrace. But mostly he looks so beautiful in these photos, a gift after all these years, a beauty that I knew finally when I was in my forties in Tucson. I am alive, fully in the moment, in a time that comes across to me now after years of being lost.

What would have happened if my mother and father had let the dog live? I think no one ever looked at me like this dog, lying off to the side of me, not pressing on me, but ever there and knowing fully where I was. I was in love. And there we were, together, caught in about thirty shots, and I am alive as I would never be in any photo that my father took after that time, during the years in Atlanta when I was made into something that was never who I was. I became an approximate self. I was only what could be appropriated. They tried to tame me, with a poodle who humped and a Pekingese who posed, and I wore lace dresses and ruffles. No more plain cotton. But cramped in corners, up on the bed, or stripped down to my slip on a sofa, trying, always trying to be in another world, where dog tags could be worn out in the field of war, or misery could be shown, worn out and desperate, though only six or seven years old. Ready to be wrapped up like a lady and worn like an accouterment to my mother who drank, went out late at night, and yelled at my father, whose only power remained, transmuted in the final impression of the print, down

They Killed My Dog   47

there in the darkroom in the basement. But that other world, I discover now, is a time long ago and forgotten, with a hound I now see who sat beside me and let me be whatever I was, just then, as we looked out at the world, not quite motionless, moored precariously in an earth, animated, looking for some faith in life that was sufficient.

I AM NOT SURE WHERE MY FATHER bought the painting that I have kept with me for over twenty years now. Done in the early 1950s, the painting reminds me of the stern simplicity of Giovanni de Paolo, its background measured and its burnished orange applied with restraint. A white dog sits turned toward a table. Hungry, its mouth open in a kind of grin, the dog stares into the distance. A fish so long that it covers most of the table's surface lies there dead. It is quite beautiful, lying so still on a bed of greens. Like an offering, to the viewer, to the dog, the fish on the table is framed as if on stage, with a dull red curtain pulled clear on either side to reveal the promise of food, a meal neatly prepared. The artist's signature, "Peterson Laurent," boldly done, appears in black paint, written after the words "St. Marc, Haiti." He was born in Saint-Marc, Haiti, on the coast near the Artibonite, though his life and death are mysterious. He is not usually mentioned along with other painters of the so-called Haitian Renaissance, heralded by DeWitt Peters when he founded the Centre d'Art in 1944: Philomé Obin and his brother Sénèque, Rigaud Benôit, Castera Bazile, Wilson Bigaud, and Adam Leontus. Nor did Peters ask him to work on the murals of Holy Trinity Cathedral along with Obin, Bazile, Bigaud, and others, including Toussaint Auguste, Gabriel Lévêque, and Préfète Duffaut. Completed in 1951, Holy Trinity Cathedral, known simply as Le Cathédral, was destroyed in the earthquake of 2010. In Ute Stebich's *Haitian Art*, her catalog of the show at the Brooklyn Museum that opened in 1978, I search through the painters' biographies with their birth dates or birth and death dates. Only Laurent bears the strange designation after his name "active 1940–1958." What happened to him? "All we know about Peterson Laurent is that he was apparently a railroad black-smith and that he lived and died in St. Marc." I always remembered the story I heard from my uncle, who once owned a Haitian art gallery in New York. "He died in the gutter. Forgotten and mad with hunger, he starved to death."

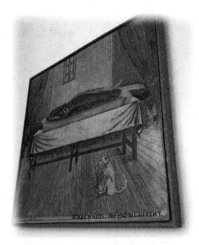

When I returned to Haiti, Laurent's dog stayed on my mind. Dogs were everywhere. In the streets or rummaging in the ravines turned into dumps strewn with garbage, running along with the goats, the chickens, and the pigs. The chickens scratch at the dirt, the pigs root in the refuse, the goats look on in a kind of wonder, while the dogs alone seem fierce with concentration and purpose. In La Gonâve the dogs look like Australian dingoes. They guard us as we sleep, barking through the night as donkeys bray and roosters crow, announcing the dawn hours before it comes. Out in the countryside, I see a dog and cannot tell whether it is living or dead. I give it a kernel of corn. He is covered in mange, as we used to say in the South, starved, nearly dead; only his eyes remain alive, searching. And what a face: its resignation becomes an assurance of peace, and I am shaken by such gentleness. Rocks are sometimes thrown at the dogs. I wince at stories of people with machetes angrily hacking their bodies into shreds if they "steal an egg," the usual excuse when a trespassing dog must be killed. No one seems to take notice of the dogs.

They are the backdrop to my return, the only thing that is constant, that I feel as if I still know. I lie down on the floor with Denise, the dog they call the "dumb one." Her mother, Blackie, is old and pregnant again. The last time she had children, she had no milk to give them, and all of them died.

There is no letup during these last few days in Port-au-Prince. Something is wrong, and I know it. I am at an upper-middle-class home in Pétionville, but I have eyes only for the dog, one of the most beautiful I have ever seen. A large Great Dane, it is a puppy who will be taught to guard the house. But for now it is left outside alone in a concrete prison, a cubicle the length of a side of the house. Left alone on the gray stone floors with nothing inside, the dog has no bed, no blankets, nothing at all. During dinner the dog haunts me. Invisible, an object of disregard, it is less cared for than the gadgets brought out and examined: a camera, an iPad, a laptop. After that evening, I realize that everywhere I go I am on the lookout for dogs. As awful as it sounds, I know that the dogs will determine how I think about what I once loved. Instead of mourning for what has been lost, I become a dog. I am the thing that brings me pain.

part two

when law comes to visit

dead dogs

EARLY ON FRIDAY MORNING, March 11, 2005, a caravan of vehicles drove from New Orleans down Louisiana Highway 89 to a home outside the city of Lafayette, where the highway meets La Neuville Road in the heart of Cajun country. State police, a SWAT team, U.S. customs officials, and other federal agents, with the aid of the Louisiana Society for the Prevention of Cruelty to Animals (LA/SPCA), the Louisiana Humane Society, and the Humane Society of the United States (HSUS), raided the home of Floyd Boudreaux. They confiscated fifty-seven American pit bull terriers and charged Boudreaux and his son Guy with fifty-seven counts of dog fighting and fifty-seven counts of animal cruelty.[1] Arrested and handcuffed, they were read their Miranda rights and locked up in Lafayette Parish Correctional Center. The dogs were loaded in a truck and driven back to New Orleans. That night the LA/SPCA began killing the dogs by injection. They did not stop until the next day. By the time the Boudreauxs were released on bail on Monday morning, their dogs had already been cremated.

The dogs were not crippled, maimed, or blind. Some had scars. Some had calluses. Most were healthy, described as "normal" on the LA/SPCA's intake forms. Nineteen of the pit bulls were puppies, less than one year old. One of them would have whelped that weekend. Wendy Wolfson, at the time a veterinarian and medical director for the LA/SPCA, is now an assistant professor in shelter medicine at Louisiana State University, a program of study heavily funded by the HSUS.[2] She testified that she conducted a hands-on exam of each animal: "We did a whole barrage of things to each dog," she said. She later testified that she found evidence of dog-fighting injuries in one or two cases so all the animals were labeled "fighting dogs."[3]

Once categorized as such, all the pit bulls were assumed to be inherently dangerous—too aggressive to live. Though they were friendly and vigorous, though there was in most cases no proof of actual fighting, the dogs were deemed "threats to the public" and could therefore be killed summarily. According to Louisiana law, "fighting dogs are declared to be contraband."[4] An arbitrary label put an end to their lives, without any recourse or appeal, without even notice to their owners. Not only were the dogs no longer personal property, but, once seized from their owners, they had become legally disposable too.

Three and a half years after the raid, in October 2008, the Boudreauxs were acquitted of all charges. If convicted, they might have faced ten years of imprisonment with or without hard labor for each count. Judge Kristian Earles found no evidence of any crime. The state's case against them was so weak that he ruled without even asking the defense to call its witnesses.[5] Floyd Boudreaux, a legendary dog man who had bred these dogs for most of his life, cried when the verdict was read. During the proceedings, the Boudreauxs' lawyer, Jason Robideaux, condemned the LA/SPCA. "The State's purpose in this case was to seize those dogs, the Boudreauxs' dogs, and kill them, and thus, end the bloodline," he said. "I don't want to speculate as to the reasons."[6]

Boudreaux's dogs were the product of two famous bloodlines: the generations-old Boudreaux line—his family hallmark since the 1930s—and the more recent "Eli Dogs," named after Eli, a two-time pit winner, bred to Boudreaux's Spook. Boudreaux had not pitted a dog in a fight since the late 1970s, when dog fighting was banned. Instead, his dogs appeared all over the United States in conformation shows and weight-pulling contests. The federal government enacted the federal dog-fighting law as part of the Animal Welfare Act in 1976, and Louisiana banned dog fighting in 1982.[7] In an interview just before the raid, a year before his seventieth birthday, Boudreaux said he had "been working with the breed for over half a century. . . . My dad had 'em before I did, and then I had 'em before I went to grade school. My son too. It's always been a family affair."[8]

Not until September 11, 2011, almost three years after the acquittal, did the LA/SPCA agree to a settlement, though it declined to comment on the terms. Father and son had sought damages for mental distress and loss of income they would have received from the sale of the dogs. They asked for about $300,000. "There's no more Boudreaux/Eli breed," Floyd said. "The mom and pop direct descendants that would not have been sold are dead. That's 100 years of breeding that's gone."[9]

IN 2009 I RETRACED that route to Lafayette, a two-and-a-half-hour drive west on Interstate 10 from New Orleans. I met Robideaux at the parish courthouse and a few hours later joined Floyd Boudreaux at the Courtyard Marriott out by the airport. I spent the rest of the day with Boudreaux, driving around in my rented car. In Broussard, a verdant suburb southeast of Lafayette, we visited "Old Doc" J. W. Lambert Jr., the veterinarian who had cared for Boudreaux's dogs from birth. He took a break for lunch so that he could talk to me. In the back of the clinic, right in the middle of the boarding kennel, we sat down in what he called his "lunchroom." "They knew what they were going to do before they picked those dogs up," he said. He kept his voice low when he told me about their "extermination": "God couldn't have created a more efficient destruction of evidence."[10]

Boudreaux and I walked by the Vermilion River, knelt in the Cathedral of St. John the Evangelist, stood by the Evangeline Oak immortalized by Longfellow on the Bayou Teche in St. Martinville, and ate a great gumbo at Prejeans Restaurant. He told me about his father and his childhood spent hunting, fishing, raising dogs, and speaking French. They lived on a houseboat on the river. But those days are long gone. "They came down from New Orleans to cause all the trouble, to change our way of life," he said. That morning the dogs were "wagging their tails, so happy to see the people who were going to kill them." The memories are fresh in Boudreaux's mind. While his family watched in tears, law enforcement, HSUS, and LA/SPCA agents "were cutting up, laughing outside the truck, taking the dogs away," he said.[11]

At dinner Boudreaux gently handed me his business card like some relic of a time gone by, as if to say "this stiff, glossy piece of paper will give you my past, remote now but once a source of pride and cause of existence." With a drawing of a cock on one side and a pit bull on the other, the words sparkled in white on the red background:

"Simple Man
Hobby Breeder"

"Still the Land of the Brave But Not of the Free"
CAJUN KENNELS
"From the Best Comes the Best"
Quality American Pit Bull Terriers
Puppies and Stud Service
Patterdales

AFTER THE RAID the LA/SPCA's Kathryn Destreza was recognized for her dedication to animal welfare and her role in the high-profile case. In February 2006 she was promoted from animal services director to director of humane law enforcement. A couple of years later she was honored with a replica of a vintage ASPCA peace-officer badge. She received special recognition from Ed Sayres, the ASPCA chief in New York, who praised her "extraordinary zeal in providing mercy to animals."[12] In February 2010 she became ASPCA regional director for the Southeast, and she is currently the director of investigations for the ASPCA. In the words of Matt Bershadker, senior vice president of the ASPCA's Anti-Cruelty Group, Destreza's previous job as regional director was to enhance the organization's "anti-cruelty initiatives and save countless animals across the country."[13] Interviewed after the destruction of Boudreaux's dogs, Destreza confessed that she had cried when the dogs were led, one by one, to room 9-5, the LA/SPCA's "euthanasia room," where they were killed by sodium phenobarbital injection. "Seeing those big dopey looks from those big brown eyes . . . I cried, yes, but I made sure not to cry in front of my staff," she said. "Even as we were loading them onto the truck, you couldn't help but think about what was eventually going to happen to them. Trying to breed another line like Boudreaux would be like trying to re-create Elvis. You can make some gold records, but there's only one Elvis."[14]

Laura Maloney, the chief executive officer of the LA/SPCA at the time of the raid, claimed that since "the dogs are bred specifically for aggression," they were too dangerous to be put up for adoption. Known for her "anticruelty initiatives," she is now the chief operating officer of the HSUS. "I have a pit bull myself. It's my favorite breed," Maloney said after killing the dogs. "But there was no way to rehabilitate a dog that has been so selectively bred for aggression toward other animals. If they were ever to get around another animal, they'd turn in a millisecond."[15] Robideaux sniffed out the privilege assumed in her defense. "If you've got the moral high ground, it's okay," he told me. "Your pit bulls have been redeemed. They get to live." Then he thought for a moment, looked hard at me, and said, "Morally superior people can euthanize dogs, and it isn't called 'cruelty.' "[16]

The case against Boudreaux was opened when Officer Jacob M. Dickinson, senior trooper of the Louisiana State Police, received a letter from a confidential informant about dog fighting at the

Boudreaux compound. He requested and got a search warrant; led the siege as case agent and arresting officer; gave Boudreaux's wife, Norma, a property evidence receipt for the dogs; and then turned the dogs over to Destreza and to "the care, custody, and control" of the LA/SPCA. He had no idea that the dogs would be destroyed, or as people prefer to say, "humanely euthanized," and certainly not before a verdict was reached at trial. He said that he learned about the fate of the seized dogs from the television news on the night of the arrests. He claimed no part in putting the dogs down: "I did not issue an order to destroy the animals seized; however, I did plan and subsequently made arrangements to house and care for these animals until the trial was completed."[17]

After the raid, Wayne Pacelle, president and CEO of the HSUS, declared, "The arrest of Floyd Boudreaux should strike a devastating blow to the underground world of dog fighting."[18] Following the acquittal, the HSUS scrubbed the boasts from its Web site. Without a guilty verdict, it could no longer brag about communal expiation in the form of canine sacrifice. But donors eager to confront such bold and bloody cruelty had already given their money.

THIS IS THE STORY of the fifty-seven dogs.

Boudreaux winced as he told me about the last time he saw them. The cruelty investigation team of the LA/SPCA had no trouble approaching the dogs, taking their photos, putting them on leashes, and loading them onto the trucks. "They were sweet," Boudreaux said. "Some were afraid. Others licked hands or wagged their tails. One female was going to whelp that weekend. They killed her, too."

It was late in the afternoon of my visit when Boudreaux gave me a typed list of his dead dogs. "Half a century of my life destroyed in one day," he said. In bold print at the top of the page were the following words: "These dogs were killed without due process March 11 & 12, 2005 by the Louisiana Society for the Prevention of Cruelty to Animals." Below were two columns, one each for males and females:

MALES	FEMALES
1. Flop	1. Michelle
2. Reno	2. Kerry
3. Ese	3. Female off of Scream Little Buddy
4. Simpleman	4. Kinky
5. 49	5. Cuz
6. Eddie	6. Scream
7. High Pocket	7. Malinda
8. 7/8 Lexus	8. Blackberry
9. Bazooka	9. Why
10. Law	10. Scuffy
11. Turbo	11. Jewel's daughter
12. Creepy	12. Scuffy's sister
13. Buddy	13. Jewel's daughter
14. Red & White	14. Bonnie
	15. Skinny
	16. Rose (2 female pups)
	17. June Bug (2 male pups)
	18. Girlfriend (house pet and National American Dog Breeders Association Weight Pull Champion and ACE)
	19. Chico's daughter
	20. Scream (2 male pups, 2 female pups)
	21. Mary (1 male pup, 1 female pup)
	22. Mikey (due the weekend of the raid)
	23. Timmie (1 male pup, 3 female pups)
	24. Jamie (2 male pups)
	25. Sassy (2 male pups)
	26. Little Twister (1 male pup)

Boudreaux also gave me color photos of his favorite dogs. "Oh, it was bad. It took me a week before I could open the gate and go out into the yard," he told me.[19] "Best female of show Boudreaux Red Rose"; "Grand Champion Badger, One of the All-Time Greats on the Show Circuit"; and "Blackberry," pictured with Guy in the show ring. Dogs on a desk, on the sofa, in the show ring, on a bed, in the backyard, with Boudreaux's grandson. One picture of a dog that has just won a weight-pulling competition and another with him posing with a trophy for best in show. At the bottom of each, Boudreaux neatly wrote: "Killed by the ASPCA March 2005." Girlfriend, a National Weight Pull champion, was his grandson's pet. She usually stayed in the house but happened to be outside that day.

Guy speaks softly as he gauges the drift of my thought: "My father didn't just raise that dog—he raised her granddad, her great granddad. They didn't just kill one dog. They killed a generation, a lifetime."

I force myself to look again at the pages and pages of intake photos of the impounded dogs. A pile of photocopies, these last images of the dogs have remained in my closet all this time. Their eyes wide and attentive, they stand muscled and quiet outside in the morning light. By the time they are in the clinic, their tails are down and back legs taut as if frozen. A dog crouches down: jaw, the whole face stiffened, staring out.

There they are. They were photographed either in Boudreaux's yard, a few standing in the dirt as if lost, or in the sterile surround of the clinic, in the examination room or photograph station, before being led to room 9-5. Some stand unsteadily on tables. Some are turned over to show their bellies or to lift their legs for examination. Others, especially the puppies, are held. The bad photos, the ones I have a hard time looking at, show dogs being pulled or dragged, leashes tight around their necks, so strained that their eyes bulge. So hard is the restraint that one dog's tongue hangs lolling out the side of his mouth, as if he is gagging. The animals are waiting to be slaughtered: they are already dead.

This photo collection was submitted as evidence along with evaluation sheets for each animal. Most were diagnosed "normal" or "healthy." Some were "scarred" or "calloused." None deserved to die. At the trial, the LA/SPCA also submitted intake and health evaluation forms for the dogs. Each dog was discussed separately, identified by numbers. Discussed one by one, each animal survived in effigy, part of an arduous if nonsensical recital that aimed to prove which dog, already dead, was a fighting dog.

When the case first reached the court—more than three and a half years after the dogs were seized and killed—the trial lasted for three days.[20] It took a long time to describe each dog. Day two of the trial was a grueling rendition of bureaucratic detail. Each question had to do with the condition of the dogs: what was found on their bodies, what could be gleaned from their behavior. Even the judge seemed exhausted by this need to document each dog, one at a time, only to dispense with them.

The court transcript is shocking to read.[21] The visuals bear no relation to the words of the veterinarian. Instead, it is as if the

numbering of the dogs, made nameless and tallied by the person who ordered their deaths, was meant to punish the Boudreauxs, to bring tirelessly before them what they had lost. We know as we follow the testimony that even though the men are accused, it is the dogs on trial. They fill the room.

The dogs. Animal control officers took the snapshots with a Polaroid camera. Terror in the long night: dogs put in plastic crates stacked high with blankets and sheets of plywood separating them, piled up in a van, and then driven nearly three hours to the LA/SPCA in New Orleans. For hours they were handled, examined, made ready to die. On the third and last day of the trial, we learn that the staff gave the dogs pet names as they prepared them for death.

Robideaux—"J Robi" to his friends—took control of the case during the cross-examination of the prosecution's main witness, Wendy Wolfson, whose task was to prove that every scar found on the dogs—or, it seemed, *any* bodily imperfections on head or tail, front or back paws—was a sure sign of dog fighting. The presence of scars, in her opinion, identified fighting dogs, which, according to Louisiana law, can be "humanely euthanized as soon as possible."[22] So Robideaux took her through the meaning and reach of scarification. A lot was at stake in the source, location, and extent

When Law Comes to Visit

of each scar, since proof of a certain kind of injury is necessary to show legally that dogs were pitted against each other. And the scars were the only evidence the state had on the dogs.

Robideaux had fought hard for over twenty years in the courts of Louisiana, first as a civil rights lawyer, then as a criminal defense attorney. Lately, as he put it, "I've been sidetracked with cases of alleged dog fighting." Then he laughed wearily and said, "Before,

only the disenfranchised could be railroaded; now anyone can be disenfranchised." He takes difficult cases, defends those who have little money and no power; he has no patience with posturing. He knows dogs, and he senses duplicity when he sees it.

So what about these scars? On the second day of the trial, Robideaux asks Wolfson to interpret their meaning for the court:

Q. How do you know that mark was put there by another dog?

A. Because when one dog bites another dog, you get punctate, and, very often, linear lesions. They show up in photographs. They also show up if you make the room dark and you can shine lights to see them. It's scar tissue, just like scars that you get on yourself, if they're deep enough.

Q. And that's only caused by a dog bite is your testimony?

A. When they're numerous and in certain spots, dog fighting is at the top of the list as far as differentials.

Q. Well, when you say "numerous," how many of these scars that you see on the leg?

A. Well, let's see. We can go to the scar chart and see what they said.

Q. Well, no, what you see. I want you to look at the photographs—

In the course of his questioning, Robideaux presses Wolfson to admit that scars might be caused by any number of things, including "puppy tussling," hunting, or locking up in the throes of breeding—pit bulls sometimes lock into each other when they mate. Or perhaps they were products of random fights, unorganized and not legally identifiable as dog fighting.[23] In dog after dog, she found no physical evidence of dog fighting. Wolfson repeatedly insists that any scar on a dog was caused by a dog bite, and that the bite occurred during a dog fight. None of the scars she identified were recent. All were more than three to five months old. Finally, Robideaux points to the murky distinction between the natural graying of older dogs and white hair caused by clusters of lesions:

Q. And do you consider white hair on a dog that's four to five years old scarring?

A. It depends. Sometimes the scar will fill in with gray hair. And sometimes they can gray from age. It just depends. You have to look at it and tell.

Q. You can tell that the gray hair was caused by a trauma versus old age?

A. Oh, yeah.

Robideaux is not convinced about her theory. Fourteen dogs later, he returns to "these gray hairs slash scars" and invites the court to join him in recognizing such dubious diagnostic practices:

Q. Doctor, did you consider gray hair on this dog's face to be healed over scars?

A. Yes, sir.

Q. Okay. Isn't it possible that the gray hair on this dog's face and muzzle just could have been caused by old age?

A. It's usually more uniform with old age. It's uniform just like a person. You don't get a line of gray.

Q. Have you seen my goatee?

A. It's uniform.

Though this exchange ends with reported "(laughter)," the word on the page sticks in the craw. Its parentheses set it off from the discouraging scene of testimony, a performance as unnecessary as it is dissembling, for the fate of the dogs had already been decided before the hundreds of photos were taken, before the exams were done, before any doctor wrote down her evaluations.

Q. Doctor, in regards to the last three dogs, Dog 38, 37C, 37B, the three-month-old, the three-month-old, the year-and-a-half-old, you've got no evidence, real evidence, physical evidence, of dog fighting. Were those three dogs also euthanized?

A. Yes, sir.[24]

By now the specious evidence of dog fighting is clear. The routine, almost absent-minded checklist of dogs—seen, judged, killed—leaves both lawyer and witness resigned to the monotony of categorization that fails to distinguish, of details that don't add up.

When we learn that the inventory of dead dogs will continue until the next morning, it comes across as both inevitable and disconcerting. The time it takes to tell the full and exact truth of how these dogs appeared to this veterinarian is exactly the time it took out there in the yard by the water buckets, by the doghouses, to collect the dogs with leash, with catch-pole, or by hand; to get them into the crates and load them onto the truck; to take them to the LA/SPCA; to take their photos, to examine them, to kill them.

The trial process is interminable; the words wear down our attention. From 9:00 A.M. to 5:00 P.M. in the courtroom and then on into the next morning, we try to hold on to our focus as we get through to the end of the testimony. By the time Wolfson leaves the stand after hours of testimony, we know somehow that everything is over. None of it is real anymore. Not the scars or the gray hairs or the claims of health or age or the evidence. The dogs are dead. Keeping this in mind, we sense the full weight of the law. A reader of these transcripts experiences the shame of prosecuting the innocent as well as the cold, shallow normalcy of such proceedings. Administrative routine makes what is unnatural, even sickening, into an unexceptional occurrence.

But the dogs bring us back to life, to a quickening sense of loss that is not sentimental. It is ultimate. You shed your history and you know in their flesh, the sight of their fur, the gaze in their eyes, the strength in their legs, and, most of all, the wonder and worry in the fullness of their bodies that what happened to them really is exceptional. Everything about them, though they are just images in black and white on a page, tells a story about us humans that is no longer abstract or distant: how we kill, when we cease to care, and what little remains in this world for us.

THE BOUDREAUXS WERE TRIED only for dog fighting; the charges of animal cruelty were dropped. The agents of the cruelty investigation team found what they were looking for in the chains that tethered the dogs, the dirty water in the buckets, the dirt on which they lay. They no doubt felt disgust at the sight of all these dogs outside in the sun, apparently left to fend for themselves. The doghouses were gone to seed. There were too many big crates scattered about. But more than anything else, the thought that these dogs were put into the pit made these kindhearted animal handlers angry. So they secured the dogs, put them in small crates, and drove them where the lights shone brightly on the hygienic floors. One or two dogs were frightened by their reflection in the glass windows, such a glare in their eyes. Was it another dog? They barked until the lights were turned on in the parking lot.

During the last day in court, Robideaux showed how the remaining bits of purported evidence were delusional hunches or deliberate lies. The so-called proof of dog fighting did not exist. Two treadmills were old castoffs: one was covered with toys and other clutter; on the top of the other appeared to be charcoal, bottled water, and possibly a weed-whacker. None of the investigators knew or seemed to care whether the treadmills were operable. The spring pole, a common and legal piece of fitness equipment allegedly used in this case to train fighting dogs, was actually a hit-a-way, a training device used by baseball players. It had a baseball on it. Only one break stick, a device inserted into the gap behind a pit bull's molars in order to break its grip on another dog should a fight break out, had bite marks. Owning a break stick does not indicate a habit of pitting one's dogs. The Boudreauxs had several bottles of steroids, all but one of which were in the chicken coop, where they housed fighting cocks.[25] Investigators confiscated a few videos, none of which proved dog fighting. One showed Floyd feeding the chickens. There was no dog-fighting pit. There was no proof that Reno, the much-touted alleged champion fighter publicized widely by the LA/SPCA, was anything but an old and much-beloved dog, the patriarch of the Boudreaux clan.

And it is here with the mention of Reno, one of the fifty-seven dogs killed, that I return to Kathryn Destreza, the woman whose last name Robideaux seems unable to pronounce, stumbling more than once only to be corrected time and again. No one in charge at the LA/SPCA claimed to know anything about who authorized the euthanasia of Reno and the fifty-six other dogs. Destreza—who handled the confiscation of the dogs, loaded them into the truck, oversaw the vet assessments, the photographing, the scar charts, still more photographing, and then the killing—claimed she did not know. By the time of the trial, she had been with the LA/SPCA for about seventeen years, moving up in the ranks from clinic receptionist to director of humane law enforcement. Though a nonprofit organization, the LA/SPCA is contracted as a public safety agent of the city of New Orleans.

On the third and final day of trial, Robideaux's cross-examination of Destreza was testy. With no "specialized training or education in regards to dogs or Animal Control," but only what he called "on-the-job skills," Destreza was asked to introduce herself: "I am certified with the Louisiana Animal Control Association, and they hold a yearly school," she said. "I am certified as a euthanasia technician for the State. I am National Animal Control Certified. I am a level three certified cruelty investigator with the Law Institute of Missouri." Robideaux mentioned the promotion she received after the Boudreaux raid. She tried to avoid discussing it, claiming to be unfamiliar with the Web site of her own organization, or, as she put it: "Not as familiar as I should be":

Q. Your picture is on the front page. Are you aware of that?
A. I'm aware of that picture, yes.
Q. And tell me if you agree with this statement: (Reading) When you stepped into your new role as Director of Humane Law Enforcement, for the Louisiana SPCA, in February 2006, "it will represent a significant move for both you and the organization."
A. That's correct.
Q. Okay. So you got promoted to Director of Humane Law Enforcement in February of 2006?
A. No, sir. It's not a promotion. It's more like a lateral move or some other move.
Q. Well, then it says that this new position will allow you to focus all of your time on tackling the many facets of animal cruelty.
A. That's correct.
Q. And have you seen this article before on the website?
A. I saw the picture.
Q. Okay. And it described your approach to these investigations as a military-style approach. Do you recall that?
A. I am very—yes. I recall that.

The publicity of the Boudreaux arrest greatly increased donations to the LA/SPCA, as does every announcement of another dog-fighting "kingpin" brought down. At trial, Destreza claimed that she didn't know anything about fund-raising. Robideaux pointed again to the Web site. Exasperated, he reminded her that as a director of this very organization, she must know that "information about the Boudreauxs' case" was "plastered all over its website." She admitted that they "do receive funding anytime something makes the news, yes." Then Robideaux upped the ante, prompting her to remember her role in that very publicity:

Q. Okay. In fact, in connection with this case, you recall being interviewed for an article by Michael Perlstein, staff writer for NOLA, N-O-L-A, called "Fighting Back"?
A. No. I don't recall it.
Q. I've got a copy of that article, and I'll ask if you recognize that or remember being interviewed by Mr. Perlstein?
A. I don't recall an interview, but clearly I was interviewed. But that's a long time ago, and I don't recall that particular interview.

So the court took a recess while she read the Perlstein interview that she claimed to have forgotten. When the cross-examination resumed, it became clear that not only did Destreza refer to "the prized Boudreaux bloodline," but she also touted the dogs as "hearty, healthy, and together valued at more than three hundred thousand dollars." Robideaux pressed on. Did she recall saying that "despite their rippling muscles, many of the dogs were calm, but scared, and even friendly"? She answered: "I remember the last part. I don't remember the 'rippling muscle' part."

But it's Reno that matters. Robideaux asked her to look at the photo, State Exhibit 42, Dog #04. I too now look through the set of photocopies, through the five pages of dogs #01, #02, and #03, until I get to Reno's three pages, his only memorial, though I want not to look at the large black dog with his head turned toward one of the handlers in one shot, standing gracefully in the yard in another, still on his chain, mouth open as he looks out comfortably toward something in the distance. No hulking heaviness here, not even when he's pictured on the hard floor of the clinic. So beautiful, the eyes with that look I am now familiar with, too wide and round as if staring at what he knows can't be good. And then the final one with Reno being led somewhere, his back facing me, head already turned away;

his body seems broken, waiting for what will take him through time to the other side.

Q. Do you recall that being the dog they referred to as "Reno"?
A. Yes.
Q. Okay. Are you aware that the SPCA veterinarian, Dr. Wolfson, found no evidence of dog fighting on Reno?
A. I'd have to look at the file.
Q. Now, Reno was euthanized, right? He was one of the dogs that the SPCA euthanized?
A. Yes.[26]

In the interview that she claims not to remember, Destreza bragged about Reno as the "grand champion" fighter and aging stud. As she explained to Perlstein, a veteran courts-and-cops reporter at the *New Orleans Times-Picayune*, she faced this legendary dog with a combination of astonishment and awe. "Just the thought of seeing a Boudreaux-bred dog on Boudreaux property was starting to blow me away," she said.[27] How convenient that Reno, like all the other dogs, was not alive to combat with the appeal of his presence the lies told about him; how grim that he did not survive to bring down the profit-making potential of such hype.

Judge Earles was not impressed. After a spirited argument by Robideaux and a rather wooden, even hollow recitation of offenses by the prosecuting attorney—alleged crimes that had been demolished during the three days of testimony—Earles granted Robideaux's motion for acquittal. Focusing on the key part of the law, which holds that a defendant must "own, possess, keep, or train a dog for purpose of dog fighting," Earles said, "I haven't been presented one shred of evidence of a witness who bought a dog for the purpose of dog fighting." He concluded with the bites on the dogs. No torn or missing ears, "some evidence of scars or lacerations"; no bite wounds, puncture wounds; none of the things necessary to prove that dog fighting had occurred. "And I think," he concluded, "that's where it fails. I think that 'has been used or intended for use in a dogfight' has not been proven."[28]

AT THE TIME OF THE ARREST, the state of Louisiana seized approximately 500 cc of anabolic steroids; a .410 J. Stevens model 39 sawed-off shotgun; $12,287 in cash—along with about a thousand other items, including computers, birth certificates, baptism certificates, Social Security cards, and property deeds. It was voluminous enough to fill a space the size of the courtroom in Lafayette. Investigators also found a couple of hundred roosters out in the back, but they could not be confiscated since cockfighting was at the time legal in Louisiana. More than three years after the invasion of the Boudreaux home, the state returned the funds with interest. The dogs were property, too. But they were also pit bulls. The dogs were not kept as evidence but instead faced death of a particularly grievous kind.

What is the rationale for such mass killing? This form of destruction promises moral uplift. It is not only buttressed by police power but also subcontracted by the state to the self-appointed guardians of animals. They in turn appeal to the compassion and the pockets of citizens. Under Louisiana law, so-called humane officers have the authority to euthanize fighting dogs seized as contraband. They have the same range of discretionary power as police officers. Legally, dogs are property, and owners can be deprived of their property without due process, or indeed any process at all, if their dogs are judged dangerous, hence contraband per se.

How is this judgment reached? When the dogs are declared "contraband per se." And how do dogs become not only outlawed goods but a real threat as well? The circular logic has an implacable beauty. Fighting dogs are contraband dogs, not subject to forfeiture but to necessary destruction. And how do we know if dogs have been fighting? Well, in the Boudreaux case we don't know. But that doesn't matter. Boudreaux was well known as a dog man before dog fighting became illegal. After that, he remained a breeder and trainer, a noted judge of conformation and weight-pulling contests whose dogs also were champions in these trials. No matter that he no longer fought dogs: alleged, "confidential" hearsay was enough. It doesn't matter that the dogs did not suit the legislative definition of "dogs used in dog fighting" in the Louisiana criminal code. Nor does it matter that they were not "a threat to the health and safety of the public." Nor does it matter that the dogs were not fighting at the time they were seized, or even, as the law demands, within forty-eight hours of "any organized dog fighting event." Nor does it matter that the dogs exhibited none of the injuries consistent with dog fighting as indicated in the statutes.[29] The judgment precedes the proof.

At least three times, Louisiana trooper Dickinson carried out what he described as "covert surveillance" of the Boudreaux compound: a simple one-floor house, a mobile trailer, a tool shed, and a yard filled with doghouses and dogs tethered by chains. On March 10, a day before the raid, he carried out his third and final inspection. It took place in a United States Customs AS 350 helicopter under the direction of the United States Customs Air Interdiction Unit in Hammond, Louisiana, in collaboration with Homeland Security, Louisiana State Police SWAT officers, and gaming agents.[30]

What did they see in this flyover? From inside the helicopter, Dickinson, the U.S. Customs pilot, the U.S. Customs special agent, and the lieutenant of the SWAT unit of the state police looked down and saw, in Dickinson's words, "approximately 25–30 pit bull dogs throughout Boudreaux's backyard." They were tethered and restrained within individual circular sandpits and doghouses in the dirt. "We noted dog fighting training equipment (e.g. fighting pit, spring pole) and numerous chicken houses and chickens," he explained. The report ends with a pit bull seen at around 10:45 A.M. "on top of the dog house on a tin roof due to standing water completely covering the area."[31] The dog on a hot tin roof was Cuz, who was known in the family for always liking to "be on top." She attracted a great deal of attention, as did the mud puddles. What the authorities saw, and recorded on video, from the helicopter was used to justify the assumption that Boudreaux participated in illegal dog fighting.

The classification of dogs as dangerous and the sacrifice of contraband, like the legal fictions associated with them, recall an older, enchanted world where voiceless and presumably mindless things were first personified and then surrendered, forfeited, or exterminated. When it comes to pit bulls, an earlier instinct for sacrifice lingers. Their treatment reveals how the law's understanding of rights is an assumption about status as well as about the meaning of property. In legal rationales, the taint and incapacity of the disenfranchised live on. The "humane" handlers who killed the Boudreaux dogs, even more than law enforcement, presented the dogs as necessarily sacrificed. But what wrong is restored, what societal need is satisfied by the dogs' death that would not be met by any other penalty against the owner?

This is a tale of dog-fighting paraphernalia—break sticks, treadmills, spring poles, pit bull magazines and videos, dogs in or on top of doghouses, a framed poem "Bull Dog," a framed pedigree chart, a sawed-off shotgun in the tool shed, steroids in a chicken coop, cocks in the yard. And neighbors who gossip. But it is also about the law. It is illegal to possess fighting dogs, and the remedy is not merely to seize but also to destroy them. In the case of Boudreaux's dogs, however, the illegality was only assumed, not proven. The striking feature in this case is the historical ballast that makes the immediate extermination of contraband dogs both necessary and inevitable.

In his opinion for the Court in *Sentell v. New Orleans and C.R. Co.* (1897), Supreme Court Justice Henry Billings Brown ruled that dogs "liable to work mischief" can be seized and destroyed without delay.[32] Allegedly "dangerous and vicious dogs" call for "legislation of a drastic nature." If they are thought to be dangerous to the safety or health of the public, and if they are thought "worthless," there is no time to wait to ascertain the actuality of such a threat. When "property" is thought "offensive or harmful," especially when owned by people judged "deleterious" to communal welfare, the "emergency may be such as not to admit of the delay essential to judicial inquiry and consideration." After all, these outlaw dogs resemble their owners. At the time of *Sentell*, the owners in mind were citizens who could not afford or refused to get such things as licenses, tags, or collars. Their dogs were not, Judge Brown said, of "the higher breeds" but "little better than a public nuisance."

In the twenty-first century, the dogs worthy of such preemptive strikes are known as pit bulls. Their owners take part in the larger crisis of waste in this country. They are groups long deemed expendable, working- and lower-middle-class citizens, rural whites, or blacks in ghettos. In their different ways, they are deemed economically useless, errant, and destitute, or at least unfit.

The "dangerous" classification of dogs may be arbitrary, but the status of the dog—or its owner—is decisive. A suspected "innate character" or "vicious propensity" stands in handily for actual wrongdoing. The language of threat and removal is not intended only against dangerous dogs, but also against humans viewed as marginal, undesirable, or aesthetically unpalatable.

Is a dead dog better off than a chained dog? I am not in an easy position, nor am I sanguine about the consequences of what the stories I tell yield up to our understanding of the limits of political life. Some of this material makes us viscerally uneasy, if not plain disgusted. The physical reaction is a good thing, perhaps, necessitated as it is by the brute facts of unequal power and status that I consider. Sometimes it is not good to be poor and white in America. When I met Boudreaux, we talked a lot about his past and the incomprehensibility of the present. "We're poor. Our house is falling down. We had saved and started remodeling when this happened." Lowering his voice and turning toward me with a smile, he thought aloud, "Humans are bad animals." I did not ask to go by his house. It somehow seemed to me like another kind of invasion. But as we passed by his street, Youngsville Road, he knew what I was thinking. "I passed by here for forty-five years," he said, "never bothered anyone, never hurt anyone, no tickets, no nothing, and now, they come in and kill all my dogs."[33]

SINCE THE MUCH-PUBLICIZED INDICTMENT of Michael Vick for dog fighting at his Bad Newz Kennels in Virginia, the ASPCA and the HSUS have led the campaign against cruelty, rescuing dogs from alleged dog-fighting operations. Once Vick's surviving dogs were saved from abuse and confiscated, however, the same HSUS, along with People for the Ethical Treatment of Animals (PETA), argued for their destruction. According to PETA spokesman Dan Shannon, "The cruelty they've suffered is such that they can't lead what anyone who loves dogs would consider a normal life."

Sanctimonious compassion heralds the extermination of animals. In her preface to the 1994 edition of *Adam's Task: Calling Animals by Name*, Vicki Hearne questioned the pretense of humane treatment, wondering "why the rise of the animal rights movement and an increased interest in 'humane' and 'not for profit' activities should coincide with and at times become indistinguishable from, relentless enforcement activities targeting dogs."[34] Self-righteous care not only justifies but also masks violence. The motto on the LA/SPCA logo reads: "UNLEASHING HEARTS SINCE 1888."

If it had not been for the last-minute intervention of Best Friends Animal Society, Vick's dogs would all have been put to death. They were saved from Vick by these animal welfare organizations, only to be condemned as fighting dogs by these same animal welfare organizations and then condemned to death on that ground. So the unsettling but necessary question remains: If a certain breed of dog, the pit bull, is killed everywhere by animal control—and by humane societies and maybe even by some dogfighters—*who gets to kill*? Does the addition of the adjective "humane" remove the fact of killing, of death itself?

What we know, without a shadow of a doubt, is that when the Department of Homeland Security in league with local police and the Humane Society of the United States and ASPCA set out to get alleged dogfighters, they also target dogs associated with that sport: the pit bull type. And they kill them after rescuing them— kill them while speaking the language of salvation. They save the victimized dogs from continued injury at the hands of men they deem predatory and depraved and then save them again from a life that would be too painful to bear—by killing them.

In November 2009, *Time* portrayed the mutilated, crippled, and blinded dogs rescued from a Missouri dog-fighting ring.[35] No longer to be feared, neither lethal nor hellish, these defeated dogs deserved our pity, or so the article suggested. They were more fortunate than the 146 pit bulls—including 60 puppies, even new-borns—seized from breeder and convicted dogfighter Ed Faron's Wildside Kennels in the mountains of North Carolina. Numerous organizations tried to adopt these dogs. They included Best Friends Animal Society in Utah, where Vick's dogs were rehabilitated and renamed "Vicktory Dogs" in spite of the HSUS and PETA's determination that they were beyond hope. Nevertheless, a superior court judge ordered Wilkes County Animal Control to destroy Faron's dogs. The judge insisted on following the advice of the HSUS.

Again the HSUS publicly endorsed the court's decision to kill the dogs, describing the "fight-crazy" instinct, the irrevocable nature of "game-bred dogs."

The collusion between humane organizations and the police in seizing and dispatching dogs, once revealed and understood for what it is, has a frightening and well-known political analog in Nazi concern for "life not worthy of being lived" and the euthanasia program of the Reich, which murdered over 100,000 incurably ill, severely disabled, criminally insane, or physically deformed people. Among well-meaning health officials, the program was known euphemistically as *Gnadentod*—"mercy killing" or "death by grace." Henry Bergh, the founder of the ASPCA, once noted, "Mercy to animals means mercy to mankind." The cliché is far from consoling.

chapter five

speaking about extinction

WRECKED, THE CLIMATE. Gone, the animals. Forgotten, the people. The expendable world, the corners of disregard, the zones of exclusion. And so wide are the walls that divide, the gates that protect.

When it comes to American pit bull terriers—as true dog people like to call the breed, not pit bulls—their days are numbered. The bloodline of dogs famous for old-time fighting gusto and endurance in the rough-and-tumble of the pit is being destroyed. Raids on alleged dog fighters have become a habit, something akin to ritual murder by the good and the mighty against the weak and the bad.

When I say "pit bull," I include American Staffordshire terriers as well as other dogs that merely look as if they might be part of the bully breed. As advocates of the breed explain, contemporary breed bans do not distinguish between them. Most generally, the dogs are considered cousins, bred from British bull and terrier combinations. The breed registered with the United Kennel Club and the American Dog Breeders Association is an American pit bull terrier; and with the American Kennel Club, an American Staffordshire terrier. But they do look different. The pit bull is leaner, slightly higher up on the legs, while the Am Staff is stockier, with the squarer—more robust—wedge head and the body lower to the ground.

The specter of outlawry tracks pit bulls, Am Staffs, and any dog categorized as a pit bull type. How does a dog, a breed, get labeled "dangerous"? Are "vicious propensities" known by a bite or simply by an alleged or a perceived ability to injure? The summary disposal of dogs branded as "dangerous," "offensive," or a "threat" to the public can be traced to the early common law and later to the range of police measures instituted ostensibly to protect community interests. "The act to regulate and license the keeping of dogs is an exercise of the police . . . and is constitutional," a Wisconsin court ruled in 1862.[1] Dogs are liable to extermination if their presence signals disturbance or danger, *even if they themselves are not dangerous.*

Out by the bayou in Louisiana or in the mountains of North Carolina or in the desert of Arizona, and especially in rural areas and small towns forgotten for their insignificance, breeding good dogs out of treasured bloodlines puts you at risk. Especially when John Goodwin, the anticruelty maverick of the Humane Society of the United States, has you in his sights. With a simple call to the hotline and a reward of $5,000 for anyone with a confirmed tip about dog fighters, it is not difficult for the HSUS to get reports of purported dog fighting or dog fighters. Once the organization gets the information, the HSUS gathers state troopers, police, SWAT teams, and other rescue authorities, and they raid the home and the yard of the breeder. Apparently the only "evidence" needed is a few dogs on chains, a break stick or two, a treadmill, and a tumbledown backyard.

Out in Picture Rocks, Arizona, northwest of Tucson, "Pat" Mahlon Patrick had been breeding pit bulls in his home off Orange Grove Road since the 1960s. The roundup of his dogs in February 2008 was especially brutal. These dogs, out of two bloodlines—Tombstone and Bolio—were taken to the Pima Animal Care Center and other undisclosed locations in Pima County. Estimates vary, but there were between 110 and 150 dogs, including puppies and pregnant mothers. All were killed less than two weeks after the seizure. I looked at old videos of Patrick's dogs on the Web and wondered at their beauty and apparent health.[2] Patrick and his partner, Emily Dennis, were charged with two counts of dog fighting and twenty-one counts of cruelty to animals. The neat accusations turned murky and contentious when defense attorneys cast doubt on veterinarians' testimony on behalf of the prosecution. The recurrent sticking point was the indeterminate and faded scars on the dogs' feet and ankles that in no way substantiated allegations of dog fighting.

After six days of testimony, Patrick and Dennis were acquitted in November 2008, a month after the acquittal of the Boudreauxs in Louisiana.[3] No amount of supposition could meet the demand for proof or convince the judge that Dennis and Patrick had knowingly sold pit bulls later used in dog fighting. The HSUS, which had accompanied Pima County Sheriff's SWAT deputies on the raid, then removed its account of the "2008 Pima County Dog Fighting Raid" from its Web site. But the celebratory words are still available elsewhere on the Web:

> With the arrests of these dog fighting kingpins, one of the most important underground dog fighting networks in the U.S. has been effectively dismantled.
>
> As a supplier of several major fighting-dog bloodlines, Patrick holds a status among professional dogfighters ranking second perhaps only to the infamous Floyd Boudreaux, who currently awaits trial on felony dog fighting charges after a 2005 raid on his Louisiana property put him out of business.[4]

But whether the men were dog fighters is not the question. What matters is whether the dogs were involved in fighting and, given the finding of a court that they were not, the decision of the Pima Animal Care Center and HSUS to euthanize all the dogs, even the newborns, eyes still shut, with the justification that they were either too damaged or "too vicious to be adoptable."[5]

The prosecution did not stop there. Two years after the raid, Pima County Attorney Barbara LaWall carried out a successful civil forfeiture case against Dennis's house and property, prime real estate in Tucson.[6] Though the criminal charges were dismissed, the civil proceedings—which thus had a lower standard of proof—were ongoing. Some states have considered bills that would allow forfeiture of property on which dog fighting has taken place. Even if owners are not convicted of a crime, that property could be declared a "nuisance."[7] The seizure and forfeit of Dennis's house in Tucson may be the first time in the United States that a residential property was forfeited to the state because of a legally unsustainable claim that dogs were bred for dog fighting in its vicinity. Like the fungal house in Leviticus or the inanimate objects surrendered to God or the king in the Middle Ages, the house accrued to itself the purported evil of the sentient beings occupying it. The press release of the Pima County Attorney's Office announced: "Yesterday, April 5, 2010, Arizona Superior Court Judge Stephen C. Villarreal found there was probable cause to believe the property, previously owned by Emily Dennis, had been used to commit felonies for financial gain, the breeding and selling of dogs for fighting, and ordered it forfeit." LaWall said, "This is a significant accomplishment and a major victory over those who abuse animals. My office will continue vigorous enforcement of the law to protect animals."[8]

"Definitions belonged to the definer—not the defined," as Toni Morrison wrote in *Beloved*. Protecting animals means killing them. If they have been saved, they cannot live. When the law comes to care about dogs and wants to triumph over abusive people, it punishes both humans and dogs. The targeting of dogs means the targeting of people. If a not-quite-right white owns a certain kind of dog, then both suffer. But it is the pit bull that must die, except for the rare and much publicized instances when an especially pitiable dog is chosen to be saved by a particularly compassionate person, usually a well-heeled white citizen.

Not just any dog can fan the flames of righteous wrath. Recall Ed Faron's dogs—146 in all, including 19 puppies that had been born following the raid—all killed by court order, even though Best Friends Animal Society, along with other rescue organizations, had offered to work to place the dogs. According to the *Winston-Salem Journal*, "Representatives of the Humane Society told the judge that the dogs should be destroyed, because they had been bred for generations to be aggressive."[9] Two weeks after the slaughter of Faron's dogs, and following widespread protests, Humane Society CEO Wayne Pacelle announced a new policy whereby all dogs seized by the organization would be evaluated as individuals, rather than purely on the basis of stereotypes and arbitrary definitions.

If you were a dog bred for the pit before the sensationalistic news media and benevolent organizations distorted the public image of the breed, what might you expect when fighting? It all depends on the individual and the conditions in which remembrance itself elicits idealized depiction. Some, especially young dog fighters, routinely mistreat their dogs. In their hands, dogs suffer disregard or worse. For other dog fighters, care for such unequivocally formidable dogs matters more than any win.

Though the days of pitting dogs in combat are vanishing fast, that history is what I acknowledge and choose to write about when I consider the fate of an old-style dog man like Floyd Boudreaux. My purpose is not to defend the permissibility of the practice, for I do not condone dog fighting. Rather, I ask whether it is the dog men who are cruel, and whether it is now time that we confront their enemies in "civilized" society. Especially powerful nonrepresentative and supralegal organizations arrogate to themselves by virtue of other people's emotionalism and prejudice the right to seize the property of innocent citizens and destroy dogs that are guilty of no crime. They do all this under cover of law. But legal language in a nonhuman terrain, too often accompanied by moralistic and modifier-laden expressions, naturally complements the legal sleight of hand that escapes constitutional scrutiny. I am writing from the dogs' point of view, counterfactual or impossible as that may appear. What concerns me is the sacrifice of dogs, in these cases pit bulls, for the imagined sins of their human counterparts out there in the country or in the streets of our cities.

CONDITIONED FOR ABOUT TWO MONTHS before the match in that period known as the "keep," you and your human companion are close, pulled into the most intense proximity: walking, running on the treadmill, weight pulling, or just running for hours on the road. You endure together until the day of the match, and then, even then, you are together in the pit. The old Cajun rules set out the steps to take before the match: a flip of a coin to see who gets to wash his dog first and then the call to turn and scratch.[10] The dogs continue fighting until one of them makes a "turn," which is defined as turning the head and shoulders away from the opponent. The dog that made the turn must "scratch" to its opponent; the dog must cross the scratch line, which is drawn in the center of the pit, and attack the opponent within a specified amount of time, usually ten to thirty seconds. If a dog fails to scratch, the opponent is declared the winner.

In *The World of the American Pit Bull Terrier*, published in 1983, Richard F. Stratton relates the horror stories about pit bulls and the misapprehensions about *pit dog men*—he does not say *dog fighters*. He warns against fighting in the heat, but most of all he warns against keeping on with the fight once it becomes clear your dog is losing. The point is not to let your dog die but to prove its mettle, to know "which dog is gamer": "If your dog is taking a beating and still scratching, and the other dog is still scratching good, too, why get your dog killed? If he is game, he is worth keeping, and no one likes to see a dog left in too long to save."

Stratton tells the story of a handler humiliated when his opponent said: "'If you don't pick that game little dog up, I'll pick mine up, and you can have the win!' The fellow picked his dog up, too, for he knew the story would quickly make the rounds on how he got his 'win.'" Stratton explains a code of honor that is lost on the animal welfare groups that bemoan the cruelty of dog fighting but don't hesitate to deprive men of their beloved, often venerated dogs, euthanizing them by the hundreds—even if, as we have seen, the accused have not pitted dogs in half a century.

To "destroy the bloodline," Jason Robideaux argued, was the purpose of exterminating the dogs before Floyd and Guy Boudreaux went to trial. His surmise turns out not to be a tall tale but rather a deadly fact, since the dogs of famous breeders are all too readily killed, even if their cases are still pending.

There is also great cruelty against pit bulls committed by rank and rookie fighters who abuse their dogs and by other dogs. Driving down a street in New York, I saw a man beating his pit bull outside a brownstone. When I called the police, I was told, "Happens all the time. Getting the dog ready for a pit fight." That is not the world of Stratton or of the breeders I have mentioned. But the horror stories make this breed—and its companion humans—the most hated of creatures. To purge our lives of cruelty, pit bulls are banned and approved for extermination by well-meaning legislators, humane organizations, and other caring citizens. This is why Stratton ends his admonition to the human who pits a game dog that is losing with words that remain in my mind even as the world they refer to is lost: "Besides, if you are any kind of dog man at all, you will feel as close as kin to your dog, especially after all the hours you've spent together during the keep. So pick your dog up and remember the purpose of the pit. It is the proving ground for determining the best of the Bulldogs."[11]

chapter six

fable for the end of a breed

ON JANUARY 13, 2005, a jury in the United States District Court for the Western District of Pennsylvania convicted Robert Stevens on three counts of violating U.S. Code Title 18 Section 48.[1] He had sold a documentary of old dog fights, one video showing dogs hunting boar, and another with footage of Japanese pit fights. The statute used to convict him made it a federal felony to "knowingly create, sell, or possess a depiction of animal cruelty" for "commercial gain." It banned images of animals being hurt, wounded, or killed if the conduct depicted was illegal under federal or state law in either the state where the images are made or the state where they are sold or possessed.

A journalist, independent filmmaker, and authority on the American pit bull terrier, Stevens did not participate in dog fights, but he compiled and sold videotapes showing them. Well known for his book *Dogs of Velvet and Steel*[2] and for the videos of dog fighting, dog-on-pig hunting, and a training method known as *Schutzhund*, Stevens wrote numerous highly regarded articles on pit bulls in journals, including the *American Pit Bull Terrier Gazette*. In *Dogs of Velvet and Steel*, Stevens promotes the unique characteristics of the breed, explaining that he "would like the Pit

Bull to be recognized, not as an outlaw, but a respected canine." He wrote the book to help "Pit Bull owners understand and raise their Pit Bulls better."[3] He had no criminal record at the time of the arrest.

Operating from his home in rural Virginia, Stevens sold three videos to two undercover law-enforcement officers who had seen them advertised in *Sporting Dog Journal*. Two of the tapes—*Pick-A-Winna: A Pit Bull Documentary* and *Japan Pit Fights*—portrayed scenes from organized dog fights. The third video, *Catch Dogs and Country Living*, depicted a pit bull tearing off the lower jaw of a wild boar, used by Stevens as an example of how not to catch prey. In *Pick-A-Winna*, Stevens compiled historical footage filmed by others documenting pit fights in Japan—where dog fighting is legal—and in the United States during the 1960s and 1970s, when it was legal here. In the booklet accompanying *Pick-A-Winna*, Stevens reminded his viewers, "Yes, it is indeed a rough sport and again, I am not condoning it—but for those who have no idea what the foundation of our breed, what makes our dogs what they are—and what they are not—you now know."[4]

At 5:30 on a spring morning, April 22, 2003, with search warrant in hand, a SWAT team wearing black ski masks, brandishing assault rifles, shouting, and shining lights, awakened Stevens and his wife, Julie. Their house was ransacked: computers, books, magazines, and other "dog fighting accouterments" were confiscated. Stevens, sixty-three years old at the time, was arrested and tried before a grand jury in Pittsburgh, where the intentional wounding or killing of animals is illegal.

Mary Beth Buchanan, then a U.S. attorney for the Western District of Pennsylvania, appointed by George W. Bush, led the prosecution of Stevens. Known for her advocacy of sweeping police powers and punitive morality—described by journalist and author Radley Balko as "Bush's porn-hatin', Tommy Chong–persecutin', . . . jury-intimidatin'" attorney—she was a favorite of Attorney General John Ashcroft.[5] After a three-day trial, Stevens was sentenced to thirty-seven months in prison and an additional three years of supervised release, more than twice as long as the sentence served by Michael Vick, who actually staged dog fights and maimed, mutilated, electrocuted, and drowned dogs. Stevens appealed. In 2008 the Third Circuit Court of Appeals overturned the conviction as an unconstitutional violation of free speech. Arguing that section 48 creates "a criminal prohibition of alarming breadth," the judges held the statute invalid under the First Amendment.[6] The government then appealed to the Supreme Court. On April 20, 2010, in a major First Amendment ruling, the Court struck down as unconstitutionally overbroad the federal law that made it a crime to create or sell dog-fight videos and other depictions of animal cruelty. Eight of the justices were in the majority; only Justice Samuel Alito dissented.[7]

There are people who like to watch animals being tortured and killed. To the delight of sexually aroused viewers, women in short skirts and stiletto heels stamp on mice or kittens. So in 1999 Congress enacted the Depiction of Animal Cruelty Act to stop the sale and marketing of what became known as "crush videos," as well as other depictions of animal cruelty. The law made an exception for such commercial trafficking when the representations "are significant and of great import," having serious political, artistic, or other value.[8]

What is perhaps most striking about the Stevens case is the blurring of the border between species: how much these dog men are just that—a hybrid entity that becomes the object of scorn and harm, threatened with extinction. I do not mean the legendary cynanthropes, or dog men of antiquity, but rather the men who used to fight dogs or the pit bull breeders who still see themselves as guardians of a tradition of fervor and pride. That legacy of dog–human relating has little to do with the assumptions of some pet keepers who perceive pit bulls and their handlers as unacceptable.

The most maligned breed, today the pit bull is the poster dog for dog fighting, herald of criminality and drug dealing, mauler of children. But a hundred years ago, even fifty, in the lifetime of fully one-third the population of the United States, the pit bull was

America's favorite dog, known as "America's breed": RCA's Nipper (pictured head cocked while listening to "his master's voice"); Buster Brown's Tige ("That's my dog Tige, he lives in a shoe!"); Pete the Pup, a member of the Little Rascals in the *Our Gang* comedies; and the pit bull pictured on the celebrated World War I poster proclaiming: "Land of the Free, Home of the Brave." The most decorated dog in military history is Sergeant Stubby, a pit bull who fought for eighteen months in the trenches of France, saved several soldiers' lives, and captured a German spy.

After dog fighting became illegal in 1976 and breed bans proliferated in the late 1980s, Stevens hoped to preserve this history, which meant keeping recorded footage from their days of pit fighting and showing their other skills so that pit bull owners could find acceptable outlets for their dogs' strength and competitive spirit. Rather than encouraging what he described as these dogs' "gladiatorial genetics," he intended to direct "the outlaw stigma" into healthy activities such as "*Schutzhund* (the ultimate companion dog-off-lead obedience . . . tracking, and protection)," and "other healthy alternatives," such as hunting, weight pulling, and agility competition.[9]

The Court's ruling in *Stevens* came down just six months after I visited Floyd Boudreaux in Louisiana. Recognizing this as yet another case about American pit bull terriers, a man who devoted his life to the breed, a federal assault, and prosecution abetted by the HSUS and the ASPCA, I thought about the culture wars that now determine the political future of our country. Dogs outlawed and impounded or killed—and the people most affected by this increasingly popular form of "humane law enforcement"—enter the theater of political battle. But perhaps because these are relationships between dogs and humans, they are not as visible— though they are as politically charged—as fights over abortion, say, or gay marriage.

At the time of the Supreme Court decision and his "victory," Stevens remained lost in the extremes others have made of him: a thug who tortures pit bulls, according to the propaganda of the

Humane Society and the ASPCA; or, as others might see him, another heroic representative of a fast-dying, God-trusting, gun-toting, and flag-raising breed. These stereotypes are convenient. They permeate our daily lives and intensify the political boundaries between Left and Right, Democrat and Republican, liberal and conservative.

What is legally significant in the Stevens case is not whether animals have the right to be free from cruelty but whether *a depiction of animal cruelty* may be banned because it lacks *significant value* or might cause *social harm*. Though the case is explicitly about what legally matters—the First Amendment guarantee of free expression—its discursive effects suggest another subtext. The Court becomes the stage for the human need to categorize, accentuated by the matter of dog fighting. In the site of justice making, we observe not kindness toward animals but the making of stigma. Outside the circle of civilized promise—and the myths of humaneness that still beset us—remain the men and their dogs, so easily dismissed and destroyed. Here legal dispossession is applicable only to certain kinds of men with certain points of view. Persecution becomes enforceable through terms that are vague but powerful (powerful because of their vagueness), terms such as "moral outrage" and "social value."

Stevens was the first person to be tried under this law controlling depictions of animal cruelty and their interstate sale for profit. The government and the HSUS tried hard, though, to present the case as one of dog fighting, since that incites people's emotions, and the anti–dog fighting agenda makes money for HSUS and organizations like it. "This is not speech," Wayne Pacelle said. "This is commercial activity of a sickening and barbaric type."[10] But, as splendidly argued by the radically disparate individuals and organizations that wrote amicus briefs on behalf of Stevens, this case is not only about dog fighting. The amici reasoned that it is also about the First Amendment and the definition of low-value speech. Put simply, victory for the government would have meant that videos of dog fighting are unprotected by the First Amendment because their harm to society outweighs their expressive value.

According to the Supreme Court justices, the government's arguments were "startling and dangerous."[11] Dangerous not only to free speech but, more important, to anyone who depicts and sells what might to some be offensive, or not serious or significant. Why are Hollywood films—some documentary, others not—allowed but Stevens's films prohibited? John Ewing's *Hood Dawgs* ("In the Hood Only One Is Left Standing") and David Roma's *Off the Chain*, a documentary sold on the HSUS Web site, treat viewers to images from modern-day dog fights, jaws ripped off, and a dog disemboweled after a pit fight. They are permitted, but Stevens's *Pick-A-Winna*, *Japan Pit Fights*, and *Catch Dogs* are forbidden.[12]

In oral argument, Justice Sonia Sotomayor picked up this line of thinking, asking Deputy Solicitor General Neal Katyal: "Could you—could you tell me what the difference is between these videos and David Roma's documentary on pit bulls? I mean, David Roma's documentary had much, much more footage on the actual animal cruelty than the films at issue here, greater sections of the film, and more explicit." As she explains, Stevens's video did not "show the actual tearing of the jaw." Since Roma's "did much more than that, showed much more than that," she asked Katyal, "Doesn't there have to be a judgment inherent in this statute?" And then Katyal revealed how ambiguous and unbounded and contingent the prohibition was: "The line will sometimes be difficult to draw."

Drawing that line becomes even more difficult in light of the statute's exemption for depictions of animal cruelty that have "serious religious, political, scientific, educational, journalistic, historic or artistic value." What some people deem "serious" might be highly arbitrary. Testifying before the district court, I. Lehr Brisbin, a fellow of the American Association for the Advancement of Science and a senior ecologist and adjunct professor at the University of Georgia, referring to *Catch Dogs*, explained that Stevens's videos taught pit bull owners lessons in technique: "Stevens is alone in a very lonely field of those people who are telling people who own pit bulls [that] [y]ou have a responsibility to do things right, to not get the dog hurt, try not to get the pig hurt and do things with control and training." He also testified that "catching pigs with dogs is not only the most effective, but essentially the most humane way to remove pigs from certain environmentally sensitive areas."[13] But the same court instructed the jury that Stevens's films could be found to have "serious" value only if they were "significant and of great import."[14]

This unusually partisan account of justice and the verbal qualifications that accompany it ensure prosecution by what Patricia Millett, Stevens's lead attorney in the Supreme Court litigation and now a judge of the United States Court of Appeals for the District of Columbia Circuit called "the value police," who set themselves up as arbiters of taste—of what is acceptable or vulgar, of what has "expressive value" and what does not. "The notion that Congress can suddenly strip a broad swath of never-before-regulated speech of First Amendment protection and send its creators to federal prison, based on nothing more than an *ad hoc* balancing of the 'expressive value' of the speech against its 'societal costs' is entirely alien to constitutional jurisprudence and a dangerous threat to liberty," Millett argued.[15]

One of the strongest arguments against the government position is that not all images of animals being intentionally wounded or killed are categorically harmful, but the unprotected (or valueless) character of criminalized speech depends solely on either one's viewpoint or one's identity. Do you like pit bulls, angling, or hunting? Are you a Hollywood film producer or a rural dog breeder? Money and position have a lot to do with which films are judged legal, and who will be deemed criminal. According to Millett, while the Humane Society praises Roma's gruesome documentary as a "must see," it condemned Stevens's "far tamer depictions."

The dividing line in section 48, "in practice, turns not on content, but impermissibly along viewpoint or speaker-identity lines," Millett wrote. "Mr. Stevens' only crime is to look at things differently than the government and its amici do. While he joins them in opposing dog fighting, he believes that images of old-fashioned or highly regulated Japanese fights can teach people to appreciate the very special genetics and characteristics of a proud and historic breed of dog."[16]

Who is the arbiter of taste? Millett compared Stevens's videos with the similar contents of HSUS promotional materials, reminding the Court, "One need look no further than the websites of the government's animal-rights amici, which use such images to inform, educate, and raise funds," and which, by implication, exclude others from such activity. What is it about Stevens's speech that makes it so offensive, so loathsome that his depictions are unlawful? And further, and perhaps more to the point, as the Court opined, depictions of Spanish bullfighting, for example, are judged *inherently* valuable, but Japanese dog fights are not. Why does one representation have more "redeeming social value" or "serious value" than the other?

The amicus brief of the Liberty Project, the American Civil Liberties Union, and the Center for Democracy and Technology in support of Stevens urged the Court to reject the government's "novel and limitless argument" that whether speech is entitled to First Amendment protection should be based on a "categorical balancing of the value of the speech against its societal costs." This "generalized concern about 'morality'" and "particularized concern about the potential impact of speech on its hypothetical audience" would invite the targeting of "certain kinds of speech"—and certain kinds of people—"for disfavored treatment."[17]

One might contend that the government's interest in prosecution is compelling because the suffering of animals is legally relevant. Indeed, animals are worthy of protection. But in *Stevens* the argument about acceptable depiction is too broad, prejudicial, and unevenly applied to set a new course for animal welfare in jurisprudence. Most critics of the Supreme Court decision focus on the allegedly offensive nature of Stevens's videos. Though free speech is the issue that mattered to the Court, for many appalled by the final verdict, practices labeled "cruel" should trump the protections of the Bill of Rights. But the meanings of "cruelty" are in the hands of the definers and subject to variation according to geography, context, class, and historical period. I am also aware of animal rights advocacy—the exhortation for animals not to suffer at the hands of humans. Yet the story of Robert Stevens matters, too. Not because he is man and not dog but because his life and his work reveal an attachment to pit bulls, a passion for their character and their lives. The closeness between his dogs and himself is both difficult and necessary to confront.

One might also contend that certain kinds of speech, Stevens's among them, are impermissible. But the powerful amicus brief from constitutional law scholars including Bruce Ackerman, Erwin Chemerinsky, Sanford Levinson, and Laurence Tribe argued at length that Stevens's videos are not analogous to obscenity or child pornography, categories of speech unprotected by the First Amendment. They further explained that the conduct prohibited in Stevens's case is not forbidden "in a consistent manner":

> If the government makes broad and numerous exceptions to the prohibition, that is strong evidence that the interest is not compelling. Child sexual abuse is unlawful in the United States in every jurisdiction, and in all circumstances. By contrast, intentional injuries to animals are permitted in a wide range of circumstances. The most obvious example is the food industry, which kills hundreds of millions of animals annually to provide not only sustenance, but also delicacies. Despite legal limits on how animals are treated in fisheries, farms, and slaughter-houses, violence and suffering are commonplace. Another obvious example is sport. Hunters lawfully kill and injure an untold number of animals every year. If we deemed the interest in protecting animals from injury and death as truly compelling, we would not tolerate the infliction of such suffering.[18]

Even if the prohibition of the interstate commercial use of a dog-fighting video were justified, the hypocrisy in this case would be unavoidable. The singularity of the government's actions against Stevens demands that we ask what precisely makes pit bulls and dog men such as him threats to well-meaning and serious folks who might like nothing more than to boil a lobster alive at a summer dinner party. Surely, free speech "must be given at least the same weight in the balance as vanity, gastronomical pleasure, and entertainment."[19] When certain kinds of human behavior are ostracized and marginalized, claims of public morality or public welfare are deftly marshaled against the poor and the suspect. Assurances of moral vigilance or humanitarian enlightenment notwithstanding, the regulatory politics of the state and law enforcement always resurface in uneven persecution. The abstract concern with humane treatment and aversion to cruelty empowers those who sacrifice dogs and their owners to a judgment about what kind of human—and what kind of dog—is acceptable. These dogs become the medium for, and ultimately suffer from, the intimidation, control, and debasement of humans. In the decision about which depictions are allowed and for what purposes lies a deeper one about who gets to be cruel—to dogs and to humans.

Had Stevens's conviction been maintained, filmed cruelty against pit bulls would still be legal if deemed to be part of a sensational though well-meaning fight against cruelty. But the fight in its graphic horror also offers itself as commentary on a dog that has become—has been made—both victim and monster. The spectacle works wonders as the media continue to demonize pit bulls, breed bans proliferate, and the extermination of disfavored dogs continues in shelters throughout the United States.

I ADMIRED PATRICIA MILLETT'S ORAL ARGUMENT before the Supreme Court on October 6, 2009. She was one of the leading appellate attorneys in her firm, and she took Stevens's case pro bono. On April 21, 2011, I wrote congratulating her on the outcome of *United States v. Stevens* and asked whether she had Stevens's mailing address. I had read his articles on pit bulls. I knew something about his life before and after his arrest. But I could not get a copy of his book *Dogs of Velvet and Steel.*

Millett asked me why I was interested in contacting Stevens. He had good cause, she explained, to distrust people. "Can you please give me a concrete and detailed sense of what you want to speak to him about," she asked, "what the questions would likely be, and what you intend the theme of your writing to be about?" I answered immediately, explaining that my questions would have a great deal to do with Stevens's life: his work with dogs and his dedication to the breed. Also, the search warrant, his arrest, and his prosecution. I wanted his personal story, and I wanted to read his book.

For a couple of months, Stevens asked questions, and I wrote Millett the answers. He sent a couple of letters through her office, with the return address "Bob Stevens, via Patricia Millett." His first letter arrived at the end of June 2011. It was handwritten on yellow, lined paper, pages and pages torn from a legal pad. His printer was broken and his connection to the Internet fitful, but he decided to write rather than keep me waiting. He began by excusing his handwriting and the delay. "I've been a journalist since late 1970's—so I KNOW how frustrating it can be dealing with folks who don't seem to want to co-operate," he wrote. He explained somewhat apologetically that he had been hurt: he had trusted interviewers and been betrayed. So until he had a sense of my motives, Millett would be our intermediary. "I want to know you better," he wrote, "and be comfortable you won't harm me. I've been harmed a lot." One day Stevens asked for my mailing address, and sometime in August I received a letter sent from his home address. The printer had been fixed.

THERE IS A WORLD OUT THERE, neglected or abhorred by many. It lies deep in our culture. It is the habitat of spirits and animals, not men. The men know that. There is always something outside the human world. It is the world of men who believe in and pray to God, to Christ and the angels of mercy, at the same time as they fight dogs or chickens, hunt all manner of game, or run through the woods, dog head low leading the way to catch wild pig. It is hard to say what matters more to them: animality or spirituality. They are in between and exist for, with, and through the impalpable and fleshly in their midst.

Theirs is another kind of love, something close to attachment and awe. Not the love as that of the cushioned elite who live in the world of sentimental entrapment, where teacup dogs can fit in your palm and barking dogs can be silenced with a simple operation. Perhaps, as Catherine, played by Jeanne Moreau, says in François Truffaut's *Jules and Jim*, one must "reinvent" the word "love." I always understood this to mean that love needed to be exhumed, not just remade, taken out of its comfort zone and pushed beyond what could be simply comprehended. Something about viscera and blood and heat and closeness more intense than what can be easily borne. The story behind *United States v. Stevens* is a true love story, to recall Tim O'Brien's "true war story." It calls for another kind of apprehension, a subtle, apparently inauspicious insistence that we take in what comes before preconception. In this realm, binaries are inefficient. Words such as "domination," "victimization," "body," and "spirit" sit uneasily in their customary positions. No longer contradictory or opposed, the words are intermeshed one in the other in the heat of an engagement shared equally by men and dogs, a nuanced and particular passion.

Stevens was cleared of all the charges, but his name will never be cleared of the innuendo. "Even though I won the case—statements about bloody cruel pit fighting remain in the records," Stevens wrote to me. "In effect I won the right to depict horrible bloody pit fights, which I didn't do!"[20] The Supreme Court's decision concerned the unconstitutionality of the statute; Stevens's behavior was irrelevant. Stevens, his work with dogs, the devotion and commitment, that side of him that could contradict or at least question the damaging portrait trumpeted on the HSUS Web site,

"Who Is Bob Stevens?" was hidden, buried under legal arguments about the scope of the First Amendment.[21] Stevens never had the chance to talk about his infatuation, a wonder that began when he saw his first American pit bull terrier.

There was no place for any of that in the degrading aftermath of the raid on his home or during the sensational testimony in the U.S. district court where he became nothing more than criminal number 04-51. Vilified as a dog fighter filled with bloodlust and greed, he watched as the judge covered his eyes and the jury winced. Government witnesses offered impassioned if skewed allegations of dog fighting, along with images of mutilated dogs, punctured, torn, and bleeding, their suffering and death.[22] The public defender advised Stevens to take a plea bargain. His cross-examinations were cursory, and his closing statement, half a page in the court transcripts, as indifferent as a casual aside. He opposed the prosecutor with nothing more than the word "objection." He was overruled each time by the judge. The HSUS, ASPCA, and Animal Legal Defense Fund (ALDF) publicized horrific images of animal cruelty. The moral mandate of these organizations draws in the virtuous whose contempt triggers labels such as "primitive" or "bloodthirsty."

By the time an appeal reaches the Supreme Court, as anyone who works in the law knows, the details of personal experience and the complexities of earlier trials drop out, leaving only the legal ritual in its monumental authority—the Supreme Court is a place to appeal questions of law, not to relitigate questions of fact. What was at stake for Stevens, his family, and his supporters receded from view in the heady arguments about the First Amendment and hypotheticals about animal cruelty. The differences of context and scale are enormous. Yet when all is said and done, the unconditional struggle between animal rights activists and breeders, hunters, and their ilk remains, as does that between educated, urban liberals and the working poor, the hardscrabble folks called "white crackers" or "rednecks" by my parents, both immigrants and both Democrats with high-minded intentions.

What disappears, too, in this conflict is the immensity of the meeting between humans and dogs when dogs lead the way, or at least stand before us in an absoluteness that is both incontestable and overwhelming. Outside of prejudice and politics, some people live with dogs in an intimacy that demands a way of seeing so in excess of the usual that it discomfits the reasonable among us. "Do you have bulldog in you?" Stevens asked in *Pit Bull Reporter*, after his indictment on March 3, 2004. "If you really have any bulldog in you and you really care about the breed and the sport it is time to step up." To have the dog in you is to have Christ in your heart. It is not an easy place for a secular humanist to get to or identify with. But the journey to understanding matters. For here is something of a truth where there is no real clarity. Its authenticity derives from something like a spiritual texture where ambiguity is unavoidable. To see in a dog what you most want to be or attain in your daily life, to be receptive of its way of thinking, no matter how gritty, means bonding with that animal in an unusual way. Not exactly the kind of behavior we associate with caring for a pet.

Dogs take their breath at the limits of the mental and the physical. There they live out their lives suspended between themselves and their humans. Their knowing has everything to do with perception, an unprecedented attentiveness to the sensual world. They unleash intelligibility beyond the human world, beyond the resources of rational inquiry. "We still have a lot of folks who just plain do not know how animals operate and we need more animality," Stevens wrote to me just over a year into our correspondence.[23]

I pause again over the extensive archive of his e-mails. I sometimes get stuck in every detail of his being, lost in every adventure with his dogs. Perhaps this is how life insists on being remembered and known. It wasn't until I came to know Stevens and his dogs as a text that I found a way to acknowledge a world where words explain everything and nothing. I learned to know that some part of me had to question the secular and enlightened assumptions that continue to exclude the majority of people in our midst, those who know the equivocal glories of a life in faith.

I followed his dogs and risked losing myself in what was beyond my ken. Groping toward proximity with what my cohort and I have ceased to see, I wanted nothing more than to commemorate a time when animals looked at us and we followed them. What would it mean to become like a dog and in that morphing develop a bond that is like none other? It has nothing to do with sentiment. The experience of it is far from certain. To try to give a history to Stevens is also to urge asking more questions. In many ways, the person writing about a man and a world so different from her own might disconcert or, worse, arouse suspicion. To ask why he matters is also to ask why dogs matter. The answer lies in the dogs, these bull dogs. They changed my life. They also changed his.

A city boy from South Boston, Stevens received a bachelor's degree in accounting from Bentley College in 1966 and moved to Greensboro, North Carolina, where he earned a master's in business education from the University of North Carolina. After a stint in the navy, he worked as an accountant at Peat Marwick Mitchell (now KPMG). But, wanting more time for his wife and children, as well as for Morochito, the new canine member of his family, he left management for teaching.[24] Born in 1975, "Tuffy Morochito" was "named after an Argentinian boxer back in the 60s," Stevens wrote. "He was a real scrapper and was nicknamed 'Morochito,' meaning 'Sweetheart.'"[25] Stevens spent every day with Morochito—running with him (what he called "roadwork"), teaching him to track, dedicating time for obedience work, joining in roughhouse play, and, finally, giving him the rubdown, a massage that any human would be lucky to get. He read everything he could about the American pit bull terrier. He also sought out every dog man who would talk to him. "Folks, I probably shouldn't disclose some of the dumb things I've done," he wrote, "but I'll sacrifice any image I might have created of myself in order to help others."[26]

While running after the dogs and the men who knew them best, Stevens also taught advanced management and accounting at Bennett College in Greensboro. "I carried a double load," Stevens wrote me. "Bennett was an open admission all female Black College," he explained, "and my expertise was teaching those who have learning—forget the word disability—many a young girl I taught could hardly spell when I started, used street language—went on to become a C.P.A. or business executive—I had letters of appreciation." According to Stevens, most of these letters did not make it back to him when the government returned the possessions it had seized.[27]

Teaching left him enough time to begin his dog business. He spent five years writing *Dogs of Velvet and Steel*. He made his first two films about training and conditioning pit bulls, *Pit-Pro*, starring Morochito's daughter and teaching the ways of *Schutzhund*, and *The $100 Keep*. Though the latter title is taken from dog-fighting terminology, the video demonstrates conditioning and training for a conformation show in the days when pit bull bodies were supposed to be "ripped and muscular." Stevens was new to the dog world, but he caught up fast.

In Greensboro, rural pit fights were as popular as baseball games though not on most people's radar:

> This was pit dog country—home of Zebo, Red boy dogs—etc. But Greensboro citizens never knew a thing about dog matches or even that the breed existed. . . . In those days you could walk a pit bulldog on the sidewalk on a leash (except no one did) and people would ask what kind of dog is that? The public rarely saw the breed. . . . We will never return to the America of the 70s. The match dog is as much an anachronism as the American cowboy.[28]

Cowboys are gone. So are the dog men who loved with a love that was more than love, to recall Poe's lament for the dead Annabel Lee. Now brutal newcomers breed their pit bulls with larger, more aggressive dogs. They have created the human-biting pariah dogs, the "weapon dogs" that capture the imagination of law-abiding people. Stevens describes what wrecked the breed:

> For many generations, Pit Bulls have been bred to be gentle and responsive to humans but the ultimate in bravery and talent in the arena. However, when a Pit Bull is crossed with another breed they often bring out aggressiveness and often a mean temperament. These dogs can look as much a pit as the most pure bred pit champion—except they tend to be much bigger. . . . When people who desire to have a dog that everyone is afraid of and is the meanest dog on the hill, read the sensationalism about Pit Bulls—they get one and do their best to make him fulfill that image. And you can make most dogs mean if you try hard enough.
>
> In a nutshell, a combat bred Pit Bull is a small to medium sized dog that has a more affectionate personality with humans than almost any breed of dog. However they have a bravery and intelligence, forged through many generations competing as gladiators that is unparalleled in any other breed. They were bred to compete in the ring—not to be mean scary dogs that you walk around with a spiked collar to impress people who are impressed with that nonsense.[29]

The media's horrifying, blood-rousing stories of violence and abuse in the pit dog scene— gunpowder given as goad and cats fed as bait for fighting dogs with jaws so mighty they could never be pried loose from flesh—became self-fulfilling prophecies. Not only are these dogs attractive to criminals or folks who want to appear tough, but they also end up being brutalized when they refuse to eat kittens or attack people. To look back to the old days of rural dog matches, then, is to recall when dogs mattered utterly and when their promise, and the intensity that came along with it, was fulfilled in the companionship of humans who shared their lives.

Stevens's writings about Morochito and their adventures underscore their bond, a mutually invigorating and shared sentience. "I feel a very special closeness to my Pit Bull," he explained. "We've run together over hills, on forest trails, in the sweltering heat of summer, during snow storms, in the middle of rain storms—we're out on the road together. He gives me peace of mind. He's a perfect running mate. He doesn't run his mouth—can't talk; gives me time to think and clear my mind. Yeah, we've covered a lot of miles together, he and I."[30] Morochito died in 1990. Stevens lived with Morochito's progeny to the fourth generation: his daughter International Velvet; Velvet's son, International Victory; and her daughter, Victory's Secret, called "Vickie." Velvet—ornery, strong, and agile—earned a grand champion title in weight pulling, competing in the light, middle, and heavy divisions. She was "never defeated," Stevens wrote me. "Also [she was] fully Schutzhund trained and never failed to place in the conformation show ring, once earning best in show. She was also a very experienced and talented, game catch dog," who could catch a wild hog three times her weight.[31] These dogs spanned his life, marking each decade from the 1970s to Vickie's death at the end of January 2013, nearly three years after he won his freedom in the Supreme Court. She was fifteen years old.

Stevens was not sent to prison while he appealed his conviction in the district court. However, he suffered loss of his life work—not only showing dogs or training or participating in *Schutzhund* and weight-pulling competitions or dog shows but also writing or speaking publicly about dogs. He could not talk with people on the street or in a park about their dogs. He could not even appear at an event where dogs were present. The judge threatened to take Vickie away. "I was sentenced to not even speak to anyone that had a pit," he wrote me. "And—I had to not have Vickie on my property—in other words I could find another home for her." After corresponding with me for nearly three years, Stevens wrote to me about the possibility of losing her. "But—to me—she would not understand (she bonded so close to me—as a newborn every day I brought her in and put her nose on my heart and armpit to smell me holding her while I watched TV)."[32] His lackluster public defender stepped in at this point, and if it had not been for him, he would have lost, in his words, "the fourth generation dog from his Morochito." Stevens had not planned on Vickie being his last dog, but the law took care of that prospect: "Since the government closed me down I never got her bred and was not allowed to do anything with her, not even let her leave our property and now she is too old. More plans down the tubes because of the ridiculous actions on the part of our government. It really, really hurts because I so wanted my next generation to come from Vickie."[33]

These were his dogs of velvet and steel—tender and softhearted like velvet, tough and relentless like steel. His recollection captures the rhythm of pursuit and confrontation, the attentiveness and glee of human and animal, without privileging one or the other, though sentience seems most fully revealed in the animals.

> [International] Victory was a hunting dog, a warrior dog, first and foremost. . . . More than once I finally found him after a long search through the South Carolina swamps laying on the ground with a big old hog also laying on his side drained of energy while old Vic had him by the ear. . . . I've carried him on my shoulders from there to a cold creek, gone in and washed him down while he revived—and he'd continue to hunt the rest of that day and all the next. Incredible animal. . . . From the orange groves in Florida to the swamps of South Carolina, we've been through a lot together.[34]

What Stevens and other dog people call "gameness" in an animal is not aggressiveness, ill temper, or savagery, as organizations such as the HSUS claim. Gameness is an elusive trait at best, but a quick look at *Webster's Dictionary* will tell you that the adjective can mean "plucky and unyielding in spirit; resolute" or "ready and willing." Hard biters usually lack gameness, which is a will to win no matter the odds, to continue with stoicism and energy, to keep running or leaping or doing whatever it is you're doing no matter the exhaustion. Not what some folks call "sensible," these dogs are something like the aesthetes of the 1890s, bent on the bow of the absolute. They live to the fullest, infatuated with the play, the purity of being unstoppable, with the drive to get as much experience into the moment as possible. They live to the hilt, without compromise.

On a hunting day in the spring of 1998, Victory chased after something that turned out to be a black bear. Stevens found the bear but not his dog. He whacked the bear on his nose with a stick. The bear ran to a tree and climbed it. (After some years, Stevens would see the bear again: "He seemed fine, no injury on his muzzle. He didn't charge me. He didn't run away. He just snorted and lumbered past me about ten yards to my left and disappeared into the woods. Saw him often after that and called him Blackie. His progeny still come around.") When Victory returned home by himself hours later, in the dark, exhausted and cut up, Stevens knew that this was their final adventure after years of hunting together. Victory was eleven years old. From then on, instead of ranging intrepidly ahead on their jaunts in the woods as he always had, Victory stayed close to Stevens: "So I would take a break from my training and sit with him, patting that big ol' Bullyson head and talk to him about one or the other of the battles we used to have together—reminiscing."[35]

"Nobody—nobody, who has not had a real honest performance dog can feel that lump-in-the-throat love/companionship I try to describe here, but I know hundreds of readers who know exactly how I felt," Stevens writes. And in another register he laments: "Foolish animal activists will never be able to comprehend. America has so changed and it is sometimes unbearably sad—but—we move on."[36] What exactly is incomprehensible to the people who have perfected hate out of their will to care? This is not just a rhetorical quibble. In trying to live up to the memory of what we choose to forget, I write about what some of my friends and colleagues scrupulously avoid. My love for animals might be different from that of the dog man or hunter I conjure here. But pious rectitude and humanitarian judgment alarm me. It is always assumed by the free in the name of the bound, by the enlightened humanist who loathes the inarticulate or faith-bound. Stevens invites his readers to "share" in "the joys and sorrows, the high heart and heartbreak and misinformation that plagues our breed." "I write from my heart," he tells his readers, "hoping to touch yours in a search for ties that can bind rather than alienate."[37]

THOUGH STEVENS NEVER FOUGHT one of his dogs or participated in dog fighting, he respects "the traits of character, loyalty, and athletic prowess, and the traits that the breed was originally bred for hundreds of years ago." He continues: "If we are going to be forced by the laws and today's social standards into breeding a dog for looks rather than performance, in the interest of preserving the most extraordinary animal that man has ever created, let's take a good look at what the American Pit Bull Terrier is supposed to do."[38]

In his writing, within the texture of brawn and flesh and blood and what some readers will see as machismo, he probes into a kinship with animals that we have lost. "Bulldogs have taught us a lot about life," Stevens writes in an article, "Let's Talk Dogs."[39] He also bears witness to a purely inward world where mind, spirit, and, most urgently, instinct dwell together. Stevens boxed and became an expert in martial arts like pai lum kungfu and karate. He learned the "art of war" and its elusive sensitivity: "listen[ing] by feel—by sense," as he put it.[40] For him, the discipline of tai chi chuan (which he translates as "Grand Ultimate Fist"), yoga, and the life of prayer overlap with and are integral to the hunt, the old-time dog fight, and the most physical overreaching of self.

It is this embrace of paradox and contrary impulses that staves off easy judgment and the superiority that might come along with it. Stevens will not hunt deer. Perhaps he, like so many of us, grew up watching *Bambi*. I cannot say why hogs or wild boar are different, but maybe the catch-dog business is so far from what I know that I cannot comment on it. The dogs are what matter. I read again the words of I. Lehr Brisbin, who testified on Stevens's behalf. He has been capturing pigs in the wild with pit bulls since the early 1970s. These dogs do not kill. They catch and hold. "Of all the possible breeds of dogs, the pit bull has proved to my satisfaction to be the one least likely to seriously harm the pig," Brisbin writes, "so it doesn't go limping off with a dislocated or torn leg. The pit bull is essentially a flying clamp which grabs an ear and holds it until we can tie it up and take charge."[41]

Causing pain is not something most of us want to do. It is because of the pain of an animal, whether dog or pig, or any other nonhuman mammal, that I would not fight a dog or go on a hunt. But there is nonetheless something compelling about the adrenaline-pushing confrontation with a wild pig that Stevens describes with such intensity. The admiration and respect for an animal's sheer bodily strength, fierce intelligence, and courage promise a reciprocal engagement that has been lost in most human experience.

There is something else that haunts the fast-vanishing world that Stevens remembers and writes about. It is a place finally without consolation: inviolable in the uneasy tie between pain and rapture. I witnessed this in a Haitian sacrifice in the 1970s. A devotee explained to me, as the bull was led forward into the crowd, that to be given to the gods was something greatly desired, a boon that resists comparison with anything else. "You will see," he told me, "it will be smiling." Anthropomorphism reigns supreme. "I give everything to the gods I serve," he told me. "Even if I can't eat, what I have is for them." In this dubious comparison—after all, the bull is dead, the man is not—lies something tenacious about the inconsolability of religious practice and the desecration it demands. "You want to know what a pit bull feels like near the end of a match?" Stevens writes in commemoration of a hunt for a particularly remarkable wild boar in the Florida swamps. "It is like we felt."[42]

Evolving standards of decency. The worst cruelties belong to a politer world. You don't see the blood or hear the groans. Like Chief Justice John Roberts's argument for "humane" death-row execution by euthanasia in *Baze v. Rees* (2008):[43] it is decent and dignified—in other words, less upsetting to viewers. What makes it so easy for kind and cultured people to kill? To so hate pit bulls and their owners?

There is a fight on in this country, and it matters greatly to our future as people who live with animals: a fight between breeders and hunters and owners of pit bulls and the often well-heeled and collegial dog owners who condemn the cruelty of both breeding and hunting, even showing and working dogs. To take the journey with Stevens, crude or unpalatable as it might appear to some, is to know how we can reconstitute something of a life together. In the tension of our disagreements and hatreds, we might begin to share a narrative as discontinuous as it is embattled. That narrative is determined for better or for worse by our lives with dogs, and that experience somehow disables our sense of privilege and its infallible, painless cruelty.

I NEVER MET STEVENS. I had planned a visit to Windfall, his property on the edge of a lake in the Virginia countryside, but I decided not to go. Instead I look at his photos, read his words, and try to know him through them, outside of the flesh. Words written in a way that keeps sentimentality at bay, even as they insist on the enigma of feeling. "I have this symbiotic feeling for the breed," he wrote to me as I grappled with the contradictions that undergird his sensibility. "I am overly affectionate—soft-hearted. But I have a love for battle—so long as it is a game. I love wrestling, boxing—all of it. And I love to train. With a passion."[44]

Stevens's descriptions are saturated with images of the natural world. When Victory died, he lay down "sniffing the wind."[45] Far from sterile or stylized, they remain part of the voracity of his experience. Every bird, all the sounds in the country, wild turkey, red-tailed hawk, black bear, chipmunks, and squirrels, the deer he will not kill, and the names he has for his beloved cats, the cardinals, orioles, and the woodpecker "Big Bill," every last one of God's creatures. Stevens presents their shapes and brightness in arresting detail. He writes to me about "Robby the Raccoon" who has been renamed "Robin" since she lately brought her daughter around the back of their house to share "the cats' food dish and water." The raccoon he cannot kill even though it now threatens the foundations of the house. "Robin is one big pain in the neck—but so cute and endearing one can't do anything about it."[46]

THE NEW AND REVISED EDITION of *Dogs of Velvet and Steel* is a capacious achievement, moving in its honesty and impressive in its mixing of genres—history, fieldwork, memoir, and legal interpretation—written in a voice as insistent as it is unpresuming. Stevens is not exactly a polemicist. He offers himself, very much like Saint Paul in his epistles, with blemishes and qualifications. He invites us to be at ease as he moves with us through the polarities, as he draws us into unfamiliar terrain: "I have a tendency to be long-winded and often digress from the subject. . . . My general approach is to discuss Pit Bulls as though the reader and I were sitting around a campfire having a chat. Sometimes over-explain a point, but in those instances I feel the verbiage is either necessary to emphasize a point or that it is colorful."[47]

A meditation on a vanishing breed, before it is destroyed or denatured, on its past and that of its human companions, the book reconstructs for readers lives lived in the light of faith, the mind's ascent and trust in things hoped for and unseen. The photos bear witness to the unmoored playfulness of Stevens's relationship with his dogs, the pleasures of working with them, the headlong speed of a run, the rigorous conditioning and a tranquil rubdown. His swings between cogency and rambling are as dramatic as those between furtiveness and ostentation, pique and good humor. The reader's relation to this rough-and-tumble writing is further vexed by the presence of two books in the body of one, a hefty 647 pages. The most recent section acts as a prelude to the next—the entire earlier text, published in 1983, and hauled figuratively and literally into court.

The new section is as much about Stevens's suffering and stigmatization at the hands of the government as it is about the dogs he admires. Sometimes grinding in its repetition of the harms done and the losses endured, it is angry but open to the refuge offered almost as an involuntary gesture, an answer to his critics: "I do not promote antagonism against animal activists and I do not promote degradation of dog fighters. I promote a metamorphosis and honesty."[48] That candor requires telling a history that is reviled in some quarters, about dogs that took their full measure in days long gone, a time when men got down low in the dirt with their dogs and bred them not to kill but to be "warriors" and "gladiators." That is gone now, that ideal and its real costs, but Stevens wants his readers to know that past so that in this world of pampering and clickers, the pit bull can live with owners responsible and knowledgeable enough to understand what makes their dog great and special. "In order to preserve and protect the breed," as Gary Hammonds, breeder, writer, and catch-dog and conformation authority, writes in homage to Stevens, "we must educate and police ourselves . . . to save the most unique dog breed to ever live, from extinction."[49]

Stevens praises "a true bred honest-to-goodness Pit Bull":

You see there is something no animal activist or supporter of these "humane" organizations can ever comprehend. That is the feeling of awe, respect, love, and companionship one gets from owning and working with a real gladiator bred dog. . . . They will never know the feeling of owning such a surreal animal. I want to say this: I don't agree with making a dog a cutsey, poopsey, butterball. If you want me to define canine cruelty, that is it. But I don't intend to make a law that it is illegal for these folks to engage in what they believe in. I am not getting on any bandwagon over it either. They have their way with dogs and the rest of us have ours.[50]

Sitting in the living room of a neighbor's house not long ago, I was asked by a friend whether I would ever have a small dog and give up the desire for a large one; in this case, she meant my American Staffordshire terrier. "Wouldn't it be easier to have a dog that was not bred like her, who didn't require so much vigilance?" In saying those words, she seemed nearly to beckon me into a world that was not so risky, that would make me part of another world, where ownership means something else. Perhaps that's it. There is no fooling around about it. I cannot, like Vickie Hearne whom I so admire, see my way of knowing and affect in Stella's eyes. But because of that obscurity, the way every day I must "see through a glass darkly," I partake of something that is slightly not mine, where our joining together in what is sometimes mutual discomfort makes the surety of possession something torn at the edge, where anything like certainty is always gratuitous.

part three

pariah dogs

Perhaps they remembered the days of revolution in the valley, the blackened buildings, the communications cut off, those crucified and gored in the bull ring, the pariah dogs barbecued in the market place.

MALCOLM LOWRY, *UNDER THE VOLCANO*

A SOUND OF GULLS, a sunlit port, human voices, barking dogs. In a city market, dogs are walking past, lying down, sitting. Dogs gather in the center of the screen. Night falls. A dog gives birth; she nurses her babies. A constable in sharp silhouette comes and looks on as, growling, she huddles over her young. So begins Serge Avedikian's fifteen-minute animated film *Barking Island* (originally *Chienne d'histoire*), which, in 2010, won the Palme d'Or as the best short film at Cannes. The images are paintings by Thomas Azuélos, made deep and weighty, contoured yet dissolving at the edges, almost palpable.

Once the music changes, the scene shifts to humans at a long table discussing how to eliminate the dogs. Newspapers announce that there are more than sixty thousand dogs on the streets of Constantinople. The Turkish authorities appeal for an end to them. After exploring various options—gassing, incineration, turning corpses into meat for human consumption—offered by the Pasteur Institute in Paris and other European experts, the Turks decide to round up the dogs and abandon them on Sivriada (Sharp Island), a deserted place in the Sea of Marmara.

But we do not know this, not yet. We see the dogs, and we hear growls. They sense the danger. Men arrive. The bitch tries to protect her young as other dogs are grabbed, netted, and snared, dropped into wooden crates. A sputter of orange, splash of red, and the dogs overlap, catch the light or obscure its glare. Dogs crouch, or bend into the upswing of their heads, mouths open, turned toward the men who have come to get them. Touches of white, yellow, light brown, black. It is difficult to watch this gouache of light and blood, presented against the sheer shape of dogs: their firm, jagged forms, the contours of bodies. Then we see the crated dogs carried to a boat, and we hear the sound of gulls and the whimpering of dogs at sea. The whimpers become squeals as the boat nears the rock island. In a blaze of sun, in the yellow sky of the afternoon, the crates are thrown and crash against the rocks, as the dogs are left to die on crags that have no green, where nothing lives or grows.

Now, in the darkness, desperate cries are heard, while the forces of law and order, the Turkish officials, are shown in the city, sitting comfortably at their meal, these stern and approximate humans. Winds blow into the room, carrying howls and wailing. The men shut the window. In the final scene, spellbinding in its visual intensity, a cruise ship passes the island of dogs. A painter sketches the desperate and the dying, the skeletons, the dogs. Some are still alive and barking. They jump into the water and swim toward the ship. A passenger hides her eyes. Another takes photos. As the ship pulls away, the dog bodies become black specks in the water, and the sea soon covers them. But suddenly we hear the barks and, again, the howls. Is this real or a haunting memory of what had been life? A shot of the rock island, the bones, the vultures. There is not even the shadow of a dog left.

It is over. In 1910 more than thirty thousand dogs were transported to the island. An article called "Suffering Dogs: The Canine Exiles from Constantinople," written not long after their expulsion, reported:

> The death rate was about 200 a day. An industry has been started on the island by a Frenchman who skins the dead carcasses and boils them for the purpose of extracting the bones, both skin and bones being exported to Europe. Fresh arrivals at the island now take place once a week only, as the supply is fast diminishing which is not surprising, seeing that the city has been practically cleared of dogs.[1]

Avedikian links the Armenian genocide in April 1915 to these thousands of dogs cleansed from the streets of Constantinople and left to starve. Dogs were cast as perfect equivalents to those marked for displacement and death. During the film we never hear a human voice, only the dogs.

In every slaughter—and they continue today with increasing regularity—dogs alone seem prominent, present to our ears, or to our eyes. In Whistler, British Columbia, weeks after the Winter Olympics in 2010, a hundred sled dogs that had hauled tourists for a company called Outdoor Adventures were executed by the person who raised and named them.[2] In March 2011 dogs shot by animal control officers were found dead on a landfill across the street from the Chesterfield County, South Carolina, shelter.[3] Roving dogs are familiar sights in cities either in decline—like Detroit—or in full-blown gentrification—like Istanbul. On the streets of the Romanian capital, Bucharest, sixty thousand dogs face extermination, descendants of those left behind in the Communist era when residents were forced to move to urban high-rise apartments. These dogs are now being culled by court order. Euthanasia is only one option. Marcela Pisla, president of the animal rights organization Cutu-Cutu, warns, "We have seen photographs as well as videos showing dogs being killed with metal bars, electrocuted and having their throats slashed."[4] In Kiev, hunters kill street dogs with poison, or they shoot them. And as the 2014 Winter Olympics in Sochi approached, officials hired teams of exterminators to dispose of what they called "biological trash."[5]

"SOMEBODY THREW A DEAD DOG after him down the ravine."[6] The pariah dog adds the finishing touch to the death of former consul Geoffrey Firmin in the fascist Mexico of Malcolm Lowry's novel *Under the Volcano*. In J. M. Coetzee's *Disgrace*, all the dogs euthanized by Bev Shaw give sense and heft to David Lurie's gift, his service to dead dogs in post-apartheid South Africa, making him something more than human—"a dog-man: a dog undertaker; a dog psychopomp; a *harijan*." What does it mean to live, to think, in Coetzee's words, "like a dog"?[7] Why is this question so urgent? What does it mean to live in a world so depraved that to be *like a dog* is a compliment?

These questions come up unexpectedly. They intrude on my teaching William Carlos Williams. Take *Paterson* and imagine approaching Williams's language experiment, his cult of particulars, with dogs on the mind. It's not too far-fetched, since he begins with a preface that marks the shifting and speed of the poem in a way that cannot easily be put aside:

To make a start,
out of particulars
and make them general, rolling
up the sum, by defective means—
Sniffing the trees,
just another dog
among a lot of dogs. What
else is there? And to do?
The rest have run out—
after the rabbits.
Only the lame stands—on
three legs. Scratch front and back.
Deceive and eat. Dig
a musty bone

This dog is assuredly not Eliot's Jacobean dog, digging into Webster's *White Devil* to introduce the dirge of *The Waste Land*. Instead, Williams's dogs come in and out of the first three books of his long poem, scratching, peeing, and clambering at large in the park that prohibits their entry: "NO DOGS ALLOWED AT LARGE IN THIS PARK." In a poem that questions both poetic mastery and human cruelty, Williams embraces what he calls "the foulness." Fighting any cult of beauty purified of muck and mire, he affirms the presence of dogs and their particular way of knowing the world.[8]

In the park, strollers and lovers are "paced by their dogs"; a "man in tweeds" appears "combing out a new-washed Collie bitch" that "stands patiently before his caresses"; and another "walks his dog absorbedly / along the wall top—thoughtful of the dog— / at the cliff's edge above a fifty foot drop." To "unravel" a "common language" is something akin to combing a dog's hair. The burden for Williams is not just to accumulate the remnants found in the wake of insignificant lives but something riskier. Every detail, even the random marks of punctuation, abetted by an inventive profusion of things, adds to a verbal terrain that makes us think and feel and sense more abundantly than we normally do. And if there's any question that the desired entanglement of particulars, words thrown this way and that, momentary and shifting, takes its example from the life and language of dogs, we have only to hear Williams's admonition:

> Listen!   —
>> The pouring water!
>>> The dogs and trees
>> conspire to invent
>> a world—gone!
>>
>> Bow, wow!
>> . . . .
>> Bow, wow! Bow, wow!
>>
>> Variously the dogs barked, the trees
>> stuck their fingers to their noses.[9]

It all depends on the strength of the affections. Dogs bark, and trees stand along with them, though the trees hold their noses from the smell. The troubling of civility and privilege that is Williams's aim in *Paterson* depends on a subtle but raucous way of looking. Leaving no doubt about the wanton injury and casual cruelty of humankind, he digs up and puts back into the poem whatever has been ignored or cast out. With the aid of dogs yelping and their turds stinking, "Blah! / *Excrementi!* / —she spits," he surrenders his poetry to the excrescence.[10] He reminds his readers that a past of genocide and greed can be written only by depending on, even while buckling under, the force of the superfluous—or whatever the reasonable and cultivated among us identify as trash or dirt, or simply unnecessary. Such an adamant noncomposition, registering fully the perceptions of the external world, changes us physically. As real as a punch to the stomach, the writing forces us to assent to de facto subversions of good taste and propriety, so fulsomely disqualified throughout the poem.

One dog, a dead dog, becomes as crucial to the meaning of this epic as Argos is to the *Odyssey*. The lines on a dead dog form the most Homeric part of the poem, though they are introduced by an all-too-commonplace conversation about a dog bite, a dog killed, and the one who remembers his loss:

> That was your little dog bit me last year.
> Yeah, and you had him killed on me.
>
> > > (the eyes)
>
> I didn't know he'd been killed.
> > > You reported him and
> they come and took him. He never hurt
> anybody.
> > > He bit me three times.
> > > > > They come and
> took him and killed him.
> > > > > I'm sorry but I had
> to report him   .   .

> A dog, head dropped back, under water, legs
> sticking up   :
> > > a skin
> tense with the wine of death[11]

Perhaps this is how life insists on being remembered, felt, and known. Williams invokes, though tentatively, a reservoir of attachment and appetite on which all creatures draw but from which most of us have learned to cut ourselves off completely. The world comes into focus this way, with humans and dogs embroiled in a landscape of intercommunicability that might more accurately be thought of as a way of learning compassion—that is, to *bear* or *suffer with.* We might go further and consider how the embodied sentience of this poetry can be fully revealed only in what lies beyond the human. This exacerbation of life—pure sensation, the stuff of the senses—prompts us to risk losing ourselves in what is beyond our ken.

Something about death and dogs makes us think and teaches us about how we come to know and when we ought to care. The involvement of humans in the death of dogs, stray or owned, is so persistent as to leave us no way out. Reasonable slaughter, necessary removal, and enlightened euthanasia tell our history, and these dogs, judged errant and ordered dead, form the ugly reality beneath the veneer of civilization. But what matters most is that they lead us to take in what precedes or transgresses what we usually mean by understanding.

through the eyes of dogs

Like a dog
Cézanne says
that's how a painter
must see, the eye
fixed & almost
averted

W. G. SEBALD, "REMBRANDT"

HUMANS THREATEN ALL FORMS OF LIFE, including their own, and, with preconceptions as damaging as they are delusional, they wreak havoc on whatever blocks profit and its attendant chimera of progress. In a country wracked by economic collapse, ingrained racism, and political paralysis, where else is there to go, except into the eyes of dogs? To see through the eyes of dogs is to see something beneath, or outside of judgment, reason, and calculation. We need to find a way to feel the dirt and hear the breath of dogs. In shifting our stance and changing our tack, we follow their lead.

How can we begin to see from a dog's point of view, tricking our perception so that the usual conceptual distinctions do not matter? How can we feel differently without an overlay of sentimental or moralizing entrapment? As the world becomes harsher in a new global order that clears cities of the unfit or marginalized—and all for a sanitized gentrification that excludes all life that does not either consume or profit—filmmakers have turned to dogs.

At Cannes in 2014, Jean-Luc Godard's new film *Goodbye to Language* gave itself over to the senses: gorgeous landscapes, snatches of song, and, most of all, images of the dog character Roxy, who rambles, barks, and relieves himself in a breathtaking nature. The dog in the film is actually Godard's pet dog Miéville (his wife's surname). "This ends in barking," Godard says in his synopsis of the film.[1] Though critics thought Roxy might win the Palm Dog, with the gift of a collar that celebrates the top dog at Cannes, another dog—or rather dogs—won instead.

The prize went to the 250 dogs of Kornél Mundruczó's apocalyptic thriller *White God*. Two dogs, Body and Luke, play the protagonist named Hagen. Their double incarnation as pet and stray mirrors the transformation of Dr. Jekyll into Mr. Hyde. They are a mix of Labrador, German shepherd, and Shar-Pei. In this take on Samuel Fuller's *White Dog*—a story as much about the madness of racism as about the dog who experiences its effects—Mundruczó explained, "I always use dogs to symbolize minorities. I wanted to tell this tale as a metaphor about the European fears about dealing with minorities."[2] Using dogs as metaphors for oppressed peoples and making an allegory of brutal and unfortunately commonplace canine realities, Mundruczó draws viewers' attention to the human tragedy represented by the treatment of dogs. Remarkably trained by Teresa Ann Miller, these dogs—all mongrels, none pedigreed—run in a pack and take vengeance on their persecutors.

Other filmmakers, far from big-budget directors, have also turned to dogs. But not primarily as allegory for human distress; instead, their productions take dogs first and foremost for themselves, in their movement as creatures who see from a certain perspective and know differently from the people around them. Dogs become the medium for apprehending the fate of all creatures left behind in the glitz of modernization. With the onslaught of finance capitalism in places where traditions are not easily erased, the mutual entanglement between stray dogs and the humans who care for them endures. Compelled as we are to see through the eyes of dogs, our experience of such collective, relational, and unsettling life promises to foreclose a history of disregard.

How many errant dogs or errant people will be allowed to exist? That
is the question.

SERGE AVEDIKIAN

WHAT IS A DOG? What is a human? In Andrea Luka Zimmerman's film *Taşkafa: Stories of the Street* (2013), such supposed
oppositions are threatened. The filmmaking itself demands that
the viewers see something equivocal in assumptions about human
and animal, about the role of reason in making us who we are. It
delivers insights to the senses in ways that skirt and even evade
expressive communication. It is as if Zimmerman, a collaborative
and communal filmmaker, presses us to see, through a street dog's
attentiveness, something that might otherwise escape us: something that is indecipherable but also indispensable.[3]

Big words like "vengeance" and "redemption" cannot be gleaned
from watching what Zimmerman calls a "feature-length documentary essay,"[4] for she keeps close to the ground, in close contact
with the dogs that lead to her human interlocutors. We move with
them—the dogs and the city dwellers interviewed—as if film were
the only medium capable of colluding in rhythm with an experience that makes certainty somewhat illusory. We move in a slightly
obscure way toward a knowledge that is tattered at the edges.

Taşkafa premiered at the Istanbul International Film Festival
in April 2013. By May, campaigning and protests over plans for
the demolition of Gezi Park—part of Istanbul's Taksim Square—to
make way for an Ottoman-style shopping center were met with
police repression. Police fired rubber bullets and water cannons;
dogs were teargased along with people. Pictures of dogs wearing
masks and protestors helping them recover from tear gas circu-
lated over social media. I cannot forget one image of a masked dog
sleeping on her side, forming a kind of pillow for her human companion, who also slept. She appeared on tweets as "the Riot Dog
of Istanbul." Many of the street dogs, according to Zimmerman,
were "displaced, killed, blinded by the ongoing tear gas attacks."[5]
Though the government did not ultimately raze the park, the Emek

cinema and other historic buildings nearby were demolished so that a luxurious shopping and entertainment complex could be built on the site.

Against economic expedience, what Zimmerman calls "the driving impulse of our world today," *Taşkafa* explores the coexistence of humans and animals and fights the "desire to cleanse Istanbul of its non-domestic and formally untamed animal life (dogs, cats, and urban wild creatures) because they do not conform actually, or aesthetically, to the processes of gentrification." The dogs of Istanbul have been living in the streets for centuries, a part of their neighborhoods. Although Zimmerman says, "*Taşkafa* is not finally *about* dogs," in just over an hour it gets as close as possible to a document of the dog's point of view, caught in a close-up of a dog's eyes or following a dog's stride. It is *through* dogs, and their *ways of seeing*—through the remnants, and suffused with the sights or talk or sounds of all the creatures in their midst—that we learn what counts for people on the verge of losing the relationships that matter to them most.[6]

Gülen Güler, the producer of *Taşkafa*, explained to me, "I feel there's always something missing when I am in a city with no stray animals. I realize that I actually feel lonely."[7] The dogs of Galata, the old European part of Istanbul, remain in emotional and spiritual conversation with humans. Though rapidly gentrifying, the neighborhood is still an "enchanted" world, in the sense so arduously captured in the anthropologist Eduardo Kohn's *How Forests Think: Toward an Anthropology Beyond the Human*. The presence of these dogs is also political in a sense that Kohn describes: "a politics that grows not from opposition to or critique of our current systems but one that grows from attention to another way of being, one here that involves other kinds of living beings."[8]

"It was the dogs . . . they are first of all *themselves*; creatures of presence, with and amongst people, in busy streets." Exploring "the fate of such animals," Zimmerman says, "is perhaps a reminder of the violence of modernity, where all that did not belong to its idea was banished from sight." Her camera makes the connection with what is not yet lost but what we have forgotten to see. Divisions such as human and nonhuman sit uneasily in their customary positions. No longer merely contradictory or opposed, they are intermeshed in the heat of an engagement equally shared, a nuanced and particular passion. Through remarkably unobtrusive yet keenly observed interviews, Zimmerman shows how "people still, and especially now, seek to be part of a larger context, one that respects other creatures and wishes them to play a significant role in their lives."[9]

When the film begins, we hear birds and we see a dog lying on his back in a town square, feet up, head back, mouth slightly open, his shadow making light even more embodied than we can imagine. We hear the voice of John Berger reading from his novel *King: A Street Story*. He speaks as the dog, leading us into his life and that of the homeless couple he has joined in a trash-strewn wasteland at the edge of a city and on the verge of a bustling motorway. The dog's front legs move ever so slightly, like wings gliding in the air, lazily, as if to stretch off toward the heavens: "Me, if I want to look at the sky I have to do one of two things: either I put my head back, far far back into the howling position, or I lie with my legs in the air in the position of surrender. And from either of these two positions I can watch the stars and name the clouds."[10]

Then we see a shot of the tops of buildings, a port, all from the air; a long shot of a dog lying down, with two pigeons moving across the square and birds flying overhead. Birds are chirping in the background. We see a close-up of another  dog stretched out, as if flattened on the cobblestones, so still that when it lifts its head and looks into the camera, we feel a shock of recognition, but we do not yet know what we recognize, or why we should bother. But soon we learn. We are learning to look, as if for the very first time. Now we see something else: two other dogs, one small and brown, the other larger and white, are wandering across the square. A man appears and throws water at the brown dog out of a shallow bucket.

It is early morning. The city is awakening. In the bustling Beyoğlu district of Istanbul, a black dog is lying in an alley. We see men, a car moving along, then yet another dog wanders all alone, nose down, along the street of stones. Suddenly the stones become large, grainy, and slightly blurred, as we lose focus. We are walking along like the dog. Our watching becomes its walking.

Just over two minutes into the film, we hear Berger's voice again. He reads from the opening of *King*, and again he is the dog: "*I am mad to try*. I hear these words in my sleep, and when I hear them I coo like a pigeon somewhere at the back of my throat, where the gullet joins the nose. The part which goes dry when you are frightened. I am mad to try to lead you to where we live."[11] As he reads, we continue to see the stones; they move as if in synch with the dog's steps. Turning into something like sand, and whitening, they fade into indistinctness just as we hear Berger utter the words "mad to try to lead you to where we live." We are in the world of the dog, at its eye level, moving through what is no longer stone but something so spectral that it becomes palpable, as real as the sense of twilight. It is as if the most ordinary thing has become marvelous, as if the dog's footfall, though no longer seen, has led us to revel in sentience that can be apprehended only through what lies beyond human life.

Then out of the magic and into the real, we enter a world of color, with trees, the silhouette of another dog stepping down off one of the mounted slabs of concrete surrounding the park. It bounds over a spot of green and back onto the pavement. The first human language we hear—other than Berger's—is a man's words: "Come here, come, son." He bends down, and the dog seems to move just slowly enough to be petted, or, rather, touched. Then the dog bounds on, going resolutely on his own, beyond the human hands to which is attached a voice, this one exclaiming, "Shit. You little donkey!" Golden sunlight reflects off the buildings, and we are in the world again, but not as before.

The dog is Taşkafa, both a real dog and a legend on the streets of Istanbul. *Taş* means "stone" or "rock," and *kafa* means "head": Taşkafa refers to someone who is dumb, strong-willed, or stubborn. In the case of a dog, especially a street dog, it suggests strength, the will to survive. On his back with his legs up in Galata Square at the beginning of the film, now Taşkafa runs past a man called Cevat, who explains that the city authorities "sterilized him and then he lost his balance." Before that, there were other dogs that went "wherever Taşkafa went." "He was their leader. He was noble." Then Aylin, a resident interviewed for the film, speaks: "When Galata became popular, posh neighbors from posh areas started moving here. They weren't used to having the gates open. They all installed gates that closed automatically, against theft. Taşkafa slept in my building, and when I passed, I gave him something, stroked him. They had no habits like that." A couple of dogs lie on the street, deep in sleep. The city is in movement around them. The camera closes in on this threshold of flesh: black matte paw, calloused elbow, and before us the fur of dogs comes into view, balancing what we see, as if teaching us to pause in wonder before the substance of such quiescence. Taşkafa is on everyone's minds—

whether street people, shop owners, or residents, old and young. An Englishman named Bill, who early in his time in the city was accosted by dogs, learns from an inhabitant that he must be introduced to the "top dog, Taşkafa."

Now Taşkafa is dead. Three months ago, Gezgin, another local, recalls: "The municipality took him away at dawn. He died." He pauses before continuing, "Taşkafa was a beautiful animal. But he was getting old. He let people stroke him. He put his legs up. He was very smart." A shopkeeper named Bülent remembers how Taşkafa protected his store and then adds, "Not all animals take care of their babies. He was taking care of them. He didn't let others oppress him." A good judge of character, Taşkafa knew "the good people." Another person explains, "He would notice you whether you fed him or not."

In these recollections we see how fiercely inhabitants still feel his presence, as well as that of other dogs living and dead. Ömer, who has observed the street dogs for some time, says, "There were twelve dogs like Taşkafa," but when the hotel was built, "there was a guy who poisoned four of them, giving them poisoned meatballs." Taşkafa was "the king of Galata Square," Erdoğan, another person interviewed in the film, says. But for those who come to the city seeking "elegance," he adds, "The stray dog . . . destroys the whole dream, like seeing a disabled child." This dog—and there is no doubt that Taşkafa is meant to stand in for all street dogs—becomes the model of right behavior. Even when gone, he sets the conditions for a powerful, implacable consciousness that survives outside the skin of life.

Through an unusual kind of double inquiry beyond the edge of the so-called natural, Zimmerman keeps flesh and phantasm disparate but interchangeable. This is a world of matter alive with spirit, a terrain rich with things and thoughts. Replicated across the scenes of the film in multiple ways, Taşkafa possesses all the selves that ever saw or now think about him. That legacy of unconditional endurance fills the eyes, and it shapes these stories of the street with heightened life. As touching as when the dogs, their ears pricked up, turn toward a familiar voice, these human eyes are similarly affecting. Their grace owes a great deal to respect for what can never be possessed.

"As they are seen as second-class souls, they get discarded by the system, without even being noticed," Ismail, a long-time inhabitant, says. We accompany dogs that wander as if lost through the graves of a cemetery and we hear how dogs are left behind, poisoned by the municipality or disposed of, living, in the grave-yard. But devoted residents refuse to ignore these dogs, no mat-ter where they are dumped. One puppy was saved from the trash. Called Eco, he is now eight years old and a member of the family that found him.

Dogs hurrying along, sauntering, standing, or lying down become something like touchstones for an anxious humanity. As people stop their daily chores to pat their heads, to stroke or talk to them, dogs lead us to the enigma of attachment—what it means to be moved by the purely sensible order of existence. In this per-spectival tour de force, we see dogs from every vantage point: in the distance, looking out from the far end of an alley, underfoot in the square, next to one another in sleep. The dogs' eyes, ever atten-tive to the life around them, watch whatever moves, whether cars, humans, or other creatures.

In one scene, among the most moving in the film, the camera follows a large dog with full teats, as we hear Gül, a lovely woman in her forties, speak about "the history of the Ottoman times," when "there were 80–100,000 dogs. People sometimes couldn't even walk. They had to jump over them." You can't look at these dogs without remembering that past, feeling the ghosts of all the other dogs that lived on these streets. Then we  focus on a large dog and a man in the distance. They look at each other. The dog turns around and looks at the camera. As the man walks slowly away down the street, the dog stands still. When he turns again to watch the man depart, we move into a different habit of mind, where acknowledgment means more than answer-ing a command or begging for a treat. Two more dogs appear in another place on the square, basking in the sun; others walk along as if in rhythm with the people on the streets.

Taşkafa bears witness to what is left behind in the glut of modernization, tossed off as trash in a world where only profit matters. With the onslaught of greed and consumerism, the reci-

procity of street dogs and the humans that care for them persists. Neither wild nor domesticated, these dogs occupy an interme-diate space. They protect and attend to their com-panions, whether canine or not. Something like the spiritual gist of the place, these dogs also carry history in their bones. "Dogs are the ritual presence of the streets from the past," we are told. "In a sense, they are owners of this place." Never bored, they also remind inhabitants of all that is stubbornly alive and precious through a social intel-ligence that is not human. "Humans are wild," a grocer says. "We kill people, animals, and destroy nature. Is there anything more savage than that?"

I am lost in the mystery of the feet of dogs, their play and their presence in the most crowded of streets where they wait for the light to change before crossing. They wait together, looking to the

left and the right, before crossing the street, tails raised high.

Berger reads nine sections from his novel, where the dog King dreams and talks to himself. He sounds more and more like a sibylline oracle as the film proceeds, leading us from the streets of Taksim Square to the islands off the coast of Istanbul. The street dog disposal of 1910 occurred on the island of Sivriada. In the film we read the memorial to the tens of thousands of dogs "left to die and eat each other here." It reads: "After this event, people changed the name of this place from Sivriada to Hayırsızada, meaning 'the wicked island.'"[12]

A year later another attempt to rid the city of dogs failed when thousands of dogs were rescued from Sivriada. For four hundred years Istanbul's leaders have tried to get rid of the stray dogs, but, Zimmerman explains, the "city's street dogs have persisted, thanks to an enduring alliance with widespread civilian communities, which recognize and defend their right to coexist." She recalls:

> I read *King* on my first visit to Istanbul. I experienced the street dogs through this lens, one that informed my subsequent journeys there. I felt but could not initially grasp the particular sense of fellowship that informed my journey through the streets, a feeling that was/is so hard to describe, and yet one which could/can so clearly be felt. It was the dogs. We use them as metaphors, or excuses, or as the agents of a certain kind of fear, but they are first of all *themselves*; creatures of presence, with and amongst people, in busy streets.

Throughout the film the real dogs on the streets are superimposed over Berger's canine character, a kind of cinematic shadow play to the fiction. King dreams and contemplates the end of life as he once knew it. Dreams can be dangerous. And though now homeless, he speaks of his past intimacy with a couple of human strays that have been abandoned, left behind like trash and condemned to live in destitution. Zimmerman describes *King* as "a story of hope, dreams, love and resistance, told from the perspective of a dog belonging to a community facing disappearance, even erasure."[13]

The bold enmeshing of humans and dogs—and the seagulls, pigeons, chickens, and cats in their midst—requires that we suspend our beliefs and put aside our craving for final answers. In experiencing this reality, we must live in a place where neither luck nor fatality has any meaning. We learn about suffering but in a way that does not elicit pity. The experience of loss comes without the self-aggrandizing concern that says more about the one caring than about those who suffer. We learn about the unsurprising connection between pet ownership and personal prestige, between buying a purebred dog and living with a dog that is free, a creature that is neither status symbol nor property or possession. "Soon everything will be owned," a young man named Zaza laments with a smile. Some pet owners love these street dogs, but we are reminded that dogs must know their place in what he calls the "caste system": "It's like protecting your child against the doorman's children."

We learn how "sheltering," whereby administrators trust people who do not like dogs to watch over them, condemns street animals to a form of life that is worse than death. Zimmerman explained to me, "I was more interested in the (violent) gesture of sheltering (in all its meanings) instead of making a crass point."[14] Serda "the dog lover," who takes care of numerous dogs, says, "Shelters are prisons. It's not only about giving food and water." He then warns, "If a person does not care for animals . . . they are looking for a path through a desert of ice. Their feet will slip one day."

With money comes a way of relating to other living things that threatens to kill what is unique to them. Spending is like an infection that consumes whatever is in proximity to it. Though the film is too scrupulous in its reticence to make such an obvious analogy, we cannot escape the sense that waste—or, more precisely, the need to render some creatures no more than filth—inevitably comes along with lives that make value equal nothing more than money.

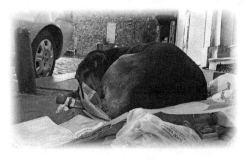

Garbage is a very real presence in the film, but not as we normally understand it. Trash becomes something other than what we think. After the neighborhoods are cleared, the money made, the cleanup and gentrification accomplished, we confront what remains, what Virgil famously called in the *Aeneid* the "tears in things" (*lacrimae rerum*). Another resident explains how "tolerance and acceptance of different styles and culture" were lost with urbanization. What is left persists as a monument to inconstancy and greed. Once in the presence of dogs, near their bodies, fur, and skin, trash becomes something like the stuff of dreams. But the real dregs remain, with the ritzy stores—Louis Vuitton is featured more than once—that signal money and the fecal motives associated with it.

TOWARD THE END OF *Taşkafa*, we are shown what the government considers the best kind of shelter for animals. Behind a fence hundreds of dogs, some on long chains, are scattered among new doghouses in a parched and desolate land. Another character, Kiran, warns viewers in one of the last interviews of *Taşkafa*, "If any of these die. . . . Dogs, animals, they all have souls. . . . I hold you responsible." Pushed out of Istanbul and dumped into forests, dogs eke out their lives beyond the usual murmurs of humans and out of their sight. Through the dogs' eyes and their exacting intimacy— fast vanishing registers of habits and dispositions—we also sense a world of humans devoid of spirit and bereft of communication.

"All dogs dream of forests," Berger writes at the beginning of *King*. Just over twelve minutes into the film, we see the dark haze of forests and hear those words. These dreams are not about the

forests to which dogs are sent by the government. We hear Berger's voice later in the film, as if his story has caught up with the reality it depicts: "Dogs should not dream. They should never dream."[15]

Taşkafa was filmed just as Turkey's Ministry of Forestry and Water was defending a controversial amendment to its animal protection law. The ministry explained: "The proposed law aims to make animals live. The aim is to prevent bad treatment of animals, clarify institutional responsibilities, and to strengthen the mechanisms of animal ownership."[16] For some the idea of *making* animals live in isolation or coercing *ownership* does not capture the attachment of persons to their neighborhood dogs. Though unowned, these dogs are with humans without being made over in their image. The ministry calls the dog preserves "natural habitat parks," "wildlife parks," or "natural life parks," but according to animal activists they are more accurately called "death camps" or "concentration camps." Without food or water and without the human contact they once knew and still seek, these dogs are left alone—free to die. We see them in Zimmerman's film, barking, running to and fro, desperately crowding, moving toward the fence, jumping, whining, forlorn, terror in their eyes.

In some cases, after neutering dogs, the city dumps them in the wilderness of the Belgrade Forest, about ten miles northeast of the city near the Black Sea. There they do anything to get to the streets again. This plan "humanely" to dispose of stray dogs recalled to many residents the removal of dogs to what some residents still call that "wicked island," the rocky haunt in the Sea of Marmara.[17]

In making *Taşkafa*, Zimmerman faced a long history of writing about the ever-present street dogs of Istanbul. Not just Mark Twain's dogs of Constantinople in *The Innocents Abroad* (1869)—which we hear about in the film—but numerous travel writers through the centuries, as well as, more recently, Orhan Pamuk, writing with a dog's voice in *My Name Is Red* (1998). Pamuk assures his readers: "Dogs do speak, but only to those who know how to listen."[18]

Unlike the vibrant sensibility embodied in *Taşkafa*, Twain's dogs are sickly and wretched scavengers. "I never saw such utterly wretched, starving, sad-visaged, broken-hearted looking curs in my life," he writes. Though they laze about, unflinching even when sheep jump and walk over them, they are not happy in their passivity: "a settled expression of melancholy, an air of hopeless despondency" hangs over them. They "sleep in the streets," undaunted in "peaceable possession of the streets" unless they are the dogs of Grande Rue, the "great street" where the hotel is, where "dogs have a sort of air of being on the lookout—an air born of being obliged to get out of the way of many carriages every day—and that expression one recognizes in a moment. It does not exist upon the face of any dog without the confines of that street. All others sleep placidly and keep no watch."[19]

Zimmerman's film ends with a return to the first appearance of Taşkafa, or rather the dog that lives on in and through her spirit. This dog is located deep in the senses of both viewers and inhabitants, part of the landscape of cities thought obsolete by stylish urbanites with their fancy-collared dogs that sport sweaters and follow along on leashes. In this glorious and fleeting scene, a bird gets stuck against a window, its wings frantically beating. We hear Berger's voice: "The bird does not believe in the glass. It thinks itself in the sky. It pauses fluttering." Time after time, it beats against the pane. We see the dog on his back, the dog we knew from the beginning. Then a "miracle" happens. Somehow the bird, blindly thrashing, finds an opening. In a breathtaking moment, "The bird knows immediately that it's back in the sky." With these words, the dog's legs become sunbeams. He turns over onto his belly, gets up, shakes off sleep, looks around, and walks away.

The street dogs of *Taşkafa* are witnesses to the lives of humans, not like Twain's lethargic creatures lying about: bits of detritus to be stepped over or avoided. The dogs of contemporary Istanbul see and feel as they roam the periphery of a city that does not welcome them. How to make sense—in the most literal meaning of sentience, in the matter of feeling—of what humans have destroyed and built up on the rubble of tradition and out of the ruin of lives?

"I can't remember if these buildings are being constructed or being taken down." It is the dog speaking. What do dogs know about place, and how do they remember what they once knew, now that they are no longer in the city but in the barren countryside, somewhere outside Istanbul? Annika Eriksson, a Swedish artist living in Berlin, filmed a ten-minute video with lots of dogs standing, playing, sniffing—all sizes of dogs and all kinds of mixed breeds exiled to a space where no one wants to be, beyond the teeming neighborhoods of Istanbul, a city that is fast erasing its past and leaving its citizens behind.[20] In *I am the dog that was always here (loop)*, the dogs are here now to speak about what has

I can't remember if these buildings are being constructed or being taken down.

gone, to recall again and again what happens to a place once familiar and now utterly changed, but which they remember so strongly
that what is gone and what lives on somehow become inextricable.

Eriksson captures in the voice-over—a speaker sounding out
words in Turkish, accompanied by English subtitles—what dogs
know, how their experiences, held tight in the mind, are played over
and over as if to perform what it means to think thought through
in a present that does not go away. Their thinking is entwined with
seeing: to remember is to attend to what roams and what stands
still, what disappears and what remains. Without their human
companions, the days are long. Nothing much breaks into their
looking. It is as close as a viewer can get to pure waiting but without
any expectation of something new coming out of the emptiness.

"All the way up to Taksim Square and round, round we go."
Four dogs, black-muzzled with short, pale fawn or tan fur, white
paws, and black or shaded ears. They look like the Kangal dog,
once the guardian of sheep in Turkey. One is sitting far from the
others, turned, looking up the road as if to see beyond the mountains. The other three stand close to one another, waiting. One
looks directly at the camera, while a second, closer to the front,
turns away, his profile before us. And one other dog, slightly bow-
legged, does not look at the camera or away but seems to be on

All the way up to Taksim Square and round, round we go.

the verge of howling, almost ready to give voice to what cannot be spoken. A lamentation. All of them stand in a great, ghostly fog, lost in the desolation around them, stilled as they recall the old connections, perhaps lingering on another kind of hope, though it appears as if forlornness as thick as it is permanent gradually encroaches, spilling over into their minds and sucking them in. They can't tell where they are or why they are here.

They are there. This is not fiction. They are real. There is something uncanny about a human voice-over in Turkish, with the subtitles in English repeating the words of loss and resignation.

Hordes of us.
All the promises. All the hopes.

Our fate is to be hidden, they say, well let's see.
Here was nothing and now I am here, we are here.
But they still feed us, but they still move us.
I've felt the winds from the Bosphorus.
We are unwanted.
I slip away.

It is as if these words were running and stamping and rearing up on the screen before being swallowed by the radiant, wet, and nearly celestial movement of dogs. Eriksson exposes the risks and the lure of anthropomorphism and the worldview so dependent on the words of nostalgia, the sense of an ego-ridden self. Once drawn into the movement of these dogs, we know that their silences and barks and gestures tell us more than any sadness usually conveyed in human language. We watch the breath and fury and flexing of life at the edges. In the extremity of its cumulative force, their lives pictured here are a call for silence. Words fail. Our language is not sufficient to the feeling, a hunger, a ravishing, something shared by all creatures, though usually not recognized.

So we watch and we feel pain, which has nothing to do with sentiment or pity. The dogs that run down the empty dirt road, in

Let's raise hell.

anticipation of what they might see and the people they might discover, dislodge us momentarily from the cruelty that has befallen them. They have just been let out of the trucks that dumped them, though we do not see the moment of disposal. We are given, moving before us, the sense of joy—what it might mean to look out and forward to what is not yet known. As viewers, we are drawn into the flutter of waste paper in the wind, a tongue licking, a dog scenting its companion's butt. It is not through language that we know what these dogs feel or want but through watching their eyes go wide, as they stop still and pause ever so quietly, turned to look away into a distance that does not end. They have one another. That is all.

Through looping and repetition, Eriksson captures the dogs' awareness of time experienced in a vacuum. The words come back again and again. But the dogs' exertions and sounds remain vibrant, as they run in the dirt or hump in the swirling dust. They circle round or run away from one another. No longer attuned to the humans whose moods they knew for such a big part of their lives, they feel something indefinable and incomplete. Perhaps they are aware of something hollow that can be filled by listening, sometimes playing, tail high and head up. But most often the emptiness is met with sitting, lying down, or staring ahead in a space wanted by no one. These are the city street dogs, no longer pausing for or stopped by humans, now going around in circles in a time without end. In the absence of that relational life, the very idea of belonging is foreclosed. We know as we watch these dogs that they are besieged. Once the very soul of the city, they are biding their time, out in the dumps. They are left to die against this desolate backdrop. But their displacement is never divorced from its cause. Through the dogs' eyes, we sense a world devoid of spirit, ravaged of communion: the high-rise developments, the spruced-up neighborhoods of the neo-Western globalized citizen.

if i sense the beauty

A dog who dies
and who knows
that he dies like a dog
and who can say
that he knows
that he dies like a dog
is a man.

ERICH FRIED, "DEFINITION"

SOME STREET DOGS DO NOT get moved beyond the city
to live in rubbish heaps. Instead, they are hunted down on the
streets. Dog slaughter is the focus of the first dozen or so minutes
of *State of Dogs*, or *Nohoi Oron* in Mongolian.[1] The film begins
with a young poet who stands before us and chants in the midst of
whines and yelps. Frantic and despairing, the cacophony of barks
comes from somewhere behind him. We do not yet see the dogs.
A blue sky appears and then the title, followed mysteriously by the
legend of the mythical dragon Rah, who comes to swallow the sun
and consume all life.

For over five weeks, I tried to watch the opening. At first I could
watch only a minute or so. Then, after other attempts, once I knew
where the dog killing began and ended, I turned the sound off and
watched that segment. Only once. Now, a couple of weeks later, I
cannot watch it at all. But I am preparing to try again.

The dogs and the hunter who guns them down are shot in real time
on a bright day in a place where such slaughter occurs regularly: Ulan

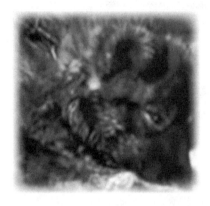

Bator, the capital of Mongolia. When the film was made in the 1990s, nearly 120,000 dogs roamed the streets of a city with about 800,000 inhabitants. Authorities decided to cull the canine population, thought to be diseased or dangerous; and so we hear from the narrator, Banzar Damchaa: "The strays bred fast and the city officials had to face the problem. They employed a hunter to clean the city. The people disliked the dog killer. They said he was an evil person. They knew that when a dog dies he was reborn as a man."[2]

What follows in the film is documentary footage of an actual dog hunter. The dogs hear the truck rumbling over the dirt. One looks out, head resting on his paws, eyes gradually opening in recognition of the threat. Another dog peers out from behind a wall. We see dogs as they hide, cower, run, or stand still, always in sight of the gun and the man with the mask. He aims and fires. There is no escape. One dog runs into the distance, but he does not get far enough. Shot once, he limps along in a kind of trot, slows down, and falls to the ground. Another dog runs up to a wall and, shot, bounces against it. A tiny dog, a great deal smaller than the others, looks up from a little blue bed that must have been put there by a resident, just for her. A black dog keeps his eye on the man,

and then, as if playing, perhaps hoping this is a game, crouches, only to know in an instant that running is his only option. He runs into a large culvert, while the hunter walks calmly over and waits for him to come out the other end.

In these first minutes of mayhem and terror, with ominous music booming in our ears, we are introduced to the dog Baasar. Based on the Mongolian belief that dogs are the last stage before humans in the endless cycle of reincarnation, the movie elaborates

on this theme, later describing him as "a Mongolian stray dog who didn't want to become a man." Then we read across the bottom of the screen: "Baasar was a clever dog and survived." We see the man with the rifle, stalking the dog with heavy step, and we are told: "But even clever dogs must learn to die." Baasar barks from behind a fence and then runs and runs, away from the killer in shots of exquisite grace with a smattering of cream and gold. Across the hellish landscape he runs and, once killed, fades into a figure of splendor, beyond any mortal doting.

What does it mean to *learn to die*? Is it the same as learning to live? And how can you die if you live in a world where the dead do not die but pass into something more than life? In this drama of life, death, and whatever lies in between, we learn, through scenes of fear, grief, and wonder, why the dog resists his rebirth as human.

Baasar is thrown out of the back of the truck, his eyes transfixed by light as he lies dying in the dump with scattered plastic bags floating on the dust like leaves. I could not watch, so I turned away again. But even though I walked out of my study and into the summer noon, I still saw his thin lips drawn

tautly back, just baring his bottom teeth. Without hesitation I murmured to myself these words from Ezekiel: "This is a lamentation and shall be for a lamentation" (19:14).

DOGS HAVE INFINITE PATIENCE. Though we think of them as creatures that seek immediate gratification—food, food, and more food—there is another level of being where dogs excel. Where the unseen or impalpable matters most, they quicken to attention. Humans make mistakes; they fumble, inexact or muddled in their communication. Have you noticed how dogs look at you and seem to accept whatever comes their way, with an understanding that seems both unexpected and satisfying? Acceptance comes in their eyes and in the way they receive us. They are so aware. They wait for us to come to them after all our petty fights, after we fall behind in work and leave them alone. They trust that eventually we will take them for that walk.

But what about street dogs that insist on knowing the humans they have lived with for such a long time but do not depend on their every look, their random attentiveness? For years I have wanted to know more about that peculiar blend of independence and need. Not need in the sense of neediness, the state of dogs attuned to the clicker, the response, and subsequent treats, but need in the way of attachment. Out of their self-sufficiency, these dogs turn toward us to be close, even if that movement forges a link that can too easily be disturbed or cruelly broken. What about the street dogs that are not always ready for a caress they might not want, not receptive to baby talk, the snuggling that means little to them? They are the last of an independent breed. This is a world that we need to know, for it is fast disappearing.

Through Baasar's memory we sense the past now lost in a changing Mongolia. Through his eyes whatever is ordinary becomes indistinguishable from the marvelous, and what we thought a fable is not exactly distinct from reality. What do dogs remember? *State of Dogs* is also about the elaborate machinery of spiritual life found where knowledge takes a turn into what is not present or past but somewhere out of life as we know it. When we learn that Baasar, as his spirit begins to wander, is not thinking or knowing like a dog any longer, we must be cautious. It does not mean that he is now like a human. He is something other than dog or human, both more and less than spirit or flesh. I like to think that he is both no longer a dog and always a dog only. How can that state be communicated to us through film?

BAASAR REMEMBERS HIS LIFE AS A SHEEPDOG, his pain when abandoned, and his struggle to survive on the streets. Though ravenous, he is aware that some city people might stone dogs or beat them, so he runs; on and on he runs. He remembers a very pregnant young woman, into whom his spirit will migrate. Her recurring appearances and his growing closeness to and love for her foreshadow the birth of a child, the human vessel for Baasar once incarnate again on earth.

No one knows for certain how many years pass. Baasar's memory, and our sense of continuity, resides in the repeated images of furred flesh, in touch or smell or taste, through the paws, and in his mind's eye on which are projected scenes from the past that soon grow faint. So strong is his desire for life that he travels long distances into what happened before his death. His spirit shaken with recognition, he sees how many different ways the rain pours, how people celebrate the end of the cold, the intertwining of sunlight and shadow in this slowly drifting world. Running along the airport road, he remembers how important it was to people, so proud that they planted trees beside it. The narrator tells us, "They wanted the trees to grow fast, so they put the body of a dead dog underneath each single tree, to make it strong and beautiful."

Sinking into his past, Baasar observes the way his ideas, like shadows formed and reformed on the landscape, hover over the lovely spectacle of the steppe slowly coming into focus. Camels, sheep, horses, goats, and then Baasar himself, tumbling in play with someone in his human family, listening to their voices, watching them—the heavy boots, lovely colored coats bulging over the garments underneath—his eyes sensing a kind of heartache increased by the worn fabric of past time.

Shot on super 16 millimeter, without a cinematographer, the film yokes us to its composition, as if we are meant to be part and parcel of its making. We are drawn into its mysteries. In its lingering semiabstract shots and slow pans, the film records two kinds of memory: dog recollection and human repetition. When they coincide—as they are meant to, sometimes through cinematic language alone—memory merges with imagination and flights of fancy with the yoke of fact. Faces and landscapes are entangled in camera movements that capture in stringent paradox the formal qualities of a convulsing civilization. Rites and rituals can appease or ward off the smoke, litter, and traffic, the ruin of soil and dirtying of skies, the polluting of waters that recall years of Soviet Communist dictatorship and betoken the onset of neoliberal democracy and the market economy that is its ready accomplice.

We see the blue of heaven and we sense the reverence of an old faith, as if the filmmakers want to remind viewers of a time of prayer, an older space of faith when Mongolian herders prayed to the great spirit on high Munkh Khukh Tengri (Eternal Blue Sky). The shots of blue and sky take us for a moment out of the dust of dead dogs, their scattered bones, and scenes of nature gone awry through a human world of greed and acquisition. A full solar eclipse that occurred in 1997 begins and ends the film. The filmmakers, the Belgian Peter Brosens and the Mongolian Dorjkhandyn Turmunkh, take up the news of the natural phenomenon so that it intertwines with the fate of Baasar, whose reincarnation is to occur on the day of the eclipse.[3] As so often happens with real events in *State of Dogs*, facts merge fluidly into invention, natural occurrence into supernatural vision. Even such unreal phenomena, however, can lose their way in the real world, as if the twilight of the gods is kindled by and inseparable from the killing of dogs. The eclipse also recalls the oldest of Buddhist legends: the dragon Rah about to bring on "eternal darkness." Dying, "Baasar could hear Rah growl and he knew that if Rah devoured the sun, then there would be no water, no sun, no moon, no life."

Each time I watched the film, I felt that threatened end to all things was already happening. It had happened in the transformation of pastoral Mongolia into the monetized sphere of debt. After decollectivization of the rural economy in the 1990s, assets that nomadic herders held in common, such as livestock, machinery, and buildings, became private property. The land, with its vast mineral deposits, turned into a resource for private ownership by less-than-virtuous foreign firms. As usual, Western conservation and development organizations, under the sign of humanitarian assistance, accelerated the destruction of traditional culture and the environment that sustained it. This commonplace narrative of corruption and collusion, dying animals and distraught herders, accompanied by a flood of foreign currency and unbridled urban development, just happens to be analogous to the mythological threat. But with one difference: whereas the dragon is forestalled before eating the sun, rapacious greed really is devouring the traditions and rights of Mongolia and its people, their animals, water, and land. It is happening right now.

Brosens and Turmunkh do not let us forget this backstory, though they are devoted to a mesmeric knowing that straightforward condemnation would defeat. Far from obvious polemic, this documentary–fiction hybrid instead gives us images that we cannot forget: Baasar guarding the sheep, looking at his family and taking them in from all possible points of view. So concentrated is Baasar's gaze in these pastoral scenes that it is as if the world dissolves into iridescent life under the weight of his devotion. These visual and sonic details allow us to know all that has been lost in the dumping of dead dogs, the belching of smoke, the growling of the power plant, the crush of cars, the shells of buildings. Yet songs and incantations, music and the vocalization of Baasar's thoughts interweave through the camera's movement. They torment us with the beauty and sound of creatures that can still feel, hear, touch,

and remember all that has been and will be destroyed.

Nomadic herders, forced to relocate on short notice, lose their animals to disease and death. Their livelihoods gone—and along with that, the intimate connection with their dogs—they find themselves in a state of confusion, groping blindly through the darkness enveloping them. Baasar's spirit revisits his time as a sheepdog, responsive to all creatures and strong in his sense of responsibility to the humans who live with him. Abandoned by the herder, who has been forced to sell his animals, Baasar roams and ultimately dies in a back alley of Ulan Bator. From the dog's-eye view, then, the apocalypse foretold in myth has already happened in reality. That fact comes to us all the more powerfully because indirectly, as if we are forced to see it more clearly, even obsessively, the more it is occluded. It is strongly felt yet somehow vague, just as prayer points to but can never incarnate the sublime. We are converted to a more difficult if less grandiose habit of mind.

One, two, three, four, five, six, seven.
I need seven reasons to die
If I'm not inspired to write an original verse
If I can't sense the beauty of low hills
If I turn my head from the red light at dawn
If I don't feel like tasting lips and breasts
If I hear alien sounds disturbing my dreams
If I'm seduced by someone else's false paradise

Or if I want to escape from this foolish life
Then I wouldn't hesitate to choose death.

One, two, three, four, five, six, seven.
I need seven reasons to live.
If I'm inspired to write an original verse
If I sense the beauty of low hills
If I enjoy the red light at dawn
If I feel like tasting lips and breasts
If there are no alien sounds disturbing my dreams
If I'm not seduced by someone else's false paradise
Or if I want to live this foolish life.
One, two, three, four, five, six, seven hundred years.
You can see me anywhere, anytime.
I am here now.
I am nowhere.

Who is this poet who stands, reciting poems directly to the camera? Do his words mean anything at all? Can they count for more than the barks that begin softly, increasing with every line he speaks? They become louder and louder, the sound of terror and alarm, somewhere invisible now, behind the poet. Entangling his language with their utterance, at the back of the buildings and sky, dogs are the cinematic backdrop to this incantation, as well as the key to its message.

We know that besides being a poet, Nyam Dagyrantz, who wrote what he intones, is also production manager of *State of Dogs*. Some reviewers have scarcely treated his incantation at the beginning of the film, since perhaps it seems nothing more than yet another eccentric appeal in a film that trades on sensory overload and random, sometimes dreamlike digressions.[4] Time is not, we know from the beginning, something that can be known only as past, present, or future. Instead, "thrown between past and present," Baasar wanders, taking us back and forth between life and death, herding us through the sluice of "time present and time past," to recall T. S. Eliot's "Burnt Norton." Experiencing the current of time, we soon lose any sense of progression. It is not just that we are in a space of dream as we follow the journey of a dog's soul after death, or that we are caught in that state between death and rebirth—*the between* (Tibetan, *bardo*). But we also find in the dog spirit a capacity to understand the chaos unleashed by humans onto a land and a people—and their allies, animals, plants, and everything living, including other spirits.

Drawing heavily on their respect for the animals of the steppes, Brosens and Turmunkh surrender to the shifting shapes and inner sights of Baasar. Through the dog, at his eye level and following his voice delivered to us through the human narrator, the filmmakers push us into a difficult but transforming encounter with shamanic power that can be made potent only through what has skin, blood, and breath. The close-ups that punctuate Baasar's quest capture his spirit as he wanders out of the dump and into the world. The flesh stinks, the fur is matted with blood, but the spirit passes into

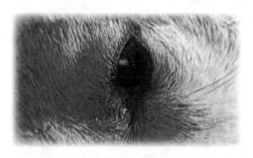

illumination: a state caught in the glare of ice, the sky still blue, the wind in his mouth. We are told, "His mind is clear." We learn from the voice in narration, "He is no longer a dog." But somehow we will be taught that he is ultimately only a dog, even as he awaits his unwished-for reincarnation as a human. We are initiated into a memory that is nothing other than actual perception: "When Baasar died, he saw a winter landscape, so bright that it was blinding. And in this landscape grew steppes and cities, beauty and cruelty, friendship and betrayal." In the mind, if we can only acquiesce in the dog's way of seeing—and remembering—even the past can be revived as what is perceivable, just as vital as before: "The most beautiful of seasons is on its way. The finest buds are breaking open," he thinks aloud.

It is a sort of feeling within ourselves, a wonder at perceiving the past anew, that *State of Dogs* demands as it visualizes Baasar's consciousness across deserts, by the sides of village roads, in the hovels outside Ulan Bator. This cinematic, wildly shifting passage through changing bodies and places undoes the fact of death. Nothing ever dies, although dead dogs abound. Yet it would be too easy to decipher what we see by resorting to only portents of shamanistic meaning. We stand instead on the threshold of an unexplored realm. Rooted in the eyes of Baasar, it takes shape as if in rhythm with his panting. The way of his remembering and the manner of his feeling command our attention even when he does not appear on the screen. The spirit of dog echoes in and through the film's visualization of all that is tactile, gradually reversing our sense of what is familiar. All parts of life emerge only through their exchange, in their translation one into the other. The seen world becomes the world of seeming, a kind of psychic enchantment, just as the mind turns into the objects once external to it.

In staying close to whatever floats before us in Baasar's perspective, we go behind the obvious, immersed in something unquantifiable. But more than that, aware of his death in the traumatic and nearly unwatchable opening scenes so commonplace in their actuality, we are prepared  to witness other metamorphoses, as well as his own impending reincarnation. Consciousness passes on from one body to another, and more particularly the lost breath of Baasar is found again as a keen laying on of matter, nothing more and nothing less than his staring upon his own "lifeless body on the rubbish dump," with fur that "smelled of blood and gunpowder." In this way a kind of mythology of rebirth can be built up inside us, out of the chaos of what remains after cruelty and torment. What Baasar calls up is not appetite but something closer to what feeling might become if it had only to do with the flush of perception, the opening light of a peculiarly intense affection. That is why his will to remember what he loved matters:

> Baasar remembered his last days as a sheepdog.
> He remembered a different kind of danger approaching.
> A danger he couldn't keep at a distance.

Watching with Baasar and the other dogs, dead or alive, gives us a way to escape the smack and dazzle of a new and wanton world where the only thing that matters is what can be bought. Although we are invited into ritual sequences of Mongolian life, making music, wrestling, eating, serving the ancestral dead, these human activities matter only insofar as they are punctuated by the presence of sheep crowding and moving across the steppe, cattle huddling in the wind, birds flying above, and, most of all, dogs running, hiding, or searching in desperation for a place to belong. Within this framework of whatever is not human or human-made, before gods and dogs, we find a respite from the mania for money, the illusion of progress, the devastation of lands, and the obliteration of lives:

> Their lives had changed from one day to the other.
> One day the Russians left the country
> The next democracy was declared
> They learned to buy and sell in a new way
> They learned to make money.
> In the new world everything was for sale.
> Only hats were left alone

even if they were lost.
Because it was believed that the
soul of a man lived in his hat.

Why do you shoot dogs? Baasar cried out.
But the people were not listening.

TO BEGIN A FILM WITH THE SLAUGHTER of dogs is a summons, a warning to the city dwellers with hardened hearts. For dogs are everywhere in Mongol lore, faithful to Genghis Khan but even more loyal to poor herders, the nomads whose lives they share. So revered are they that laws enforced and observed from the seventeenth until the twentieth century prohibited the beating or killing of dogs. When they died, they were buried high up on hills. Some say that putting them way up hindered people from walking on their remains.

Baasar, the dog of my heart's confounding, turns out to be both a real dog and the ur-dog of Mongolian legend. He hovers over all things in our experience of the film even as he recalls Tengri, the ancient and all-pervasive mystical sky deity, whose body appears as the "Great Black Dog of Heaven who was believed to be somewhere between the sun and the moon." I wrote to Brosens and asked about the opening documentary footage. I wondered whether the dog that appeared as Baasar in flashback after his killing was an individual dog, a real dog that had actually lived out on the steppes. I was tormented by the thought that somehow the filmmakers had known this dog, followed his movements from the open plains to the city. Brosens wrote: "In the beginning we introduce Baasar, then all dogs along the way become 'Baasar.' He's an archetype. Oh, do check the story of the two Mongolian dogs (usually 'Monglin hotoch nohoi') called Baasar and Haasar."[5]

The many dogs are Baasar, and they live on in folktales and legends, usually as the pair Baasar and Haasar. So much for setting him apart from those other living creatures that just happen to be dogs. They are all interconnected. The film is about a spirit of dog that does not die. The spiritual presses on us in a way that never loses touch with the matter of daily life. We too begin to travel across space and into other bodies—a state of dogs, *a condition of being dog*, not the precondition for uniqueness but rather an imperative to seek a more voracious if always provisional communion.

The inexplicable takes shape as we move through landscapes that are seen through uneven shifts in color, tonality, and flow. In its form, *State of Dogs* leads us to approach what Buddhists mean by "compassion": not sympathy but rather discernment, an insight or a striving to sense and to know what is beyond the self. Like Baasar's spirit, which never asks for pity and leaves no time or space for sentimentality, the film moves us differently. We take delight in the changeability of seasons that absorbs us as if to transform the fickle promises of humanity into something else. To watch this film demands that we train our mind to see and not see, a discipline of feeling that somehow aborts the self. It is also a matter of faith. Baasar, in taking us out of the merely human and into the unbidden grace of animality, pushes us beyond the resources of rational inquiry. The experience of such fierce and obstinate life—even in death—combats an oppressive past, along with preconceptions as damaging as they are delusional.

There are gods everywhere. Sometimes they come to us in the form of dogs, erratic and quite visible powers of all shapes and sizes, some wandering, some stuck like ghosts in the corner of a house, some hanging on as if leaves from trees, looking for another dog, or maybe human, to drop onto, stay close to, or come away with in a place beyond harm.

Death is the event that puts everything we see in the film into movement. But it is in the barks and visible presence of dogs— whether behind a fence, in the darkness, on the broad steppes in the glare of day, lying dead on the earth—that we find an anchor in the terror, a place to stand in the chaos. Finally, it is through the dead Baasar that we can best come to know the living. We know in another way. This is knowledge beyond desire or a way of happening that is finally no different from the rustling of leaves. During the summer of this writing, I saw a dead possum on the side of a road in Nashville, but it could just as well have been a dog, or any sentient being that is not of human will:

> I saw a possum dead in the road
> Curled up so peaceful back rounded
> Up against the curb paws crossed up
> Under the soft chin and thought
> That is how I want to know
> To die

coda

THE DOG OF THE CAVE

(They will say, 'Three; and their dog
was the fourth of them.' They will say,
'Five; and their dog was the sixth of them,'
guessing at the Unseen. They will say,
'Seven, and their dog was the eighth of them.'
Say: 'My Lord knows very well their
number, and none knows them, except
    a few.'
So do not dispute with them, except
in outward disputation, and ask not
any of them for a pronouncement
    on them.
And do not say, regarding anything,
'I am going to do that tomorrow'
but only, 'If God will'; and mention
thy Lord, when thou forgettest, and say,
'It may be that my Lord will guide me
unto something nearer to rectitude
    than this.')

QUR'AN, SURA 18:22–24

A DOG STRETCHES OUT HIS PAWS on the threshold of a cave.
Ashab al-Kahf. "The People of the Cave."[1] Signs shall be taken for
wonders. What does it mean to use language, and I quote Walt

Whitman from the 1855 version of *Leaves of Grass*, like "words of a questioning, and to indicate reality"?

So here lies a dog at the entrance to a cave. Whom did the dog belong to? What happened to him? We do not know. He remains unnamed, referred to merely as "their dog" (*kalbu-hum*). Given no mythical powers, he is neither demon nor gatekeeper of the realms of the dead. He is unremarkable but steady, stretched out but aware. Positioned at the opening of the cave, he guards the sleepers. In contrast with some teachings of the Prophet Mohammed, this dog appears distinct from those impure creatures—along with women and donkeys—whose presence defiles prayer.

I end with this dog story because it hints at what lies beyond human cognition. The language of this message from God, read in the translation here, comes most alive as conjecture. Tangled in its unfolding, this passage leads to a profusion of questions. Tracking its detours like a dog on the scent, we feel as if in pursuit of insights as nuanced as they are elusive.

Whether the people of the cave, who were youths when they first entered it, are three or five or seven, we do not know. Whether the dog makes their number up to four, six, or eight, we do not know. We do know that the dog is not counted as distinct from his human companions. "They will say" is repeated, but only God knows: "My Lord knows very well their / number, and none knows them, except / a few." We are left wondering what or who the other few might be, mentioned cryptically as if an afterthought.

What better way to honor the "Unseen" than to measure its mystery in asides or parentheticals? This approach to the unknowable is through the flesh, in and out of the stuff of matter. Neither moralizing nor doctrinaire, this call to truth remains hypothetical. In entering the cave, we are also brought into the realm of the negative. We find ourselves in what Kenneth Burke knew to be "the contextual ground" for "Being": the "negative," as he describes it in *The Rhetoric of Religion*.[2] Thus we read: "none knows them"; "do not dispute with them"; "and ask not any of them"; "And do not say, regarding anything." Even though the things of God are invisible, they are understood by recasting the life of the spirit as a highly sensory posture, as real as the dog or the sleepers themselves. Their bodies are turned over to the right and to the left so as not to stiffen but to remain intact as if awake and taut.

You might ask why, at the end of my book, I am preoccupied by this one passage of the Qur'an. The dog occupies a unique place here, and its significance has lived on through the centuries with multiple meanings all over the world of Islam. In commentaries it appears as, to give a couple of examples, a human reincarnated as a dog or a man in the form of a dog or a dog with human qualities. According to Ahmad ibn Muhammad al-Tha'labi in "Lives of the Prophets," "the dog was piebald with black, and his name was Qitmir." Reflecting on the color of the dog, al-Tha'labi recounts: "Ibn 'Abbas said that it was spotted; Muqatil said that it was yellow; Muhammad b. Ka'b that because of its deep redness and yellowness it shaded into red; al-Kalbi said that its color was like snow. Some said, the color of a cat; others, the color of heaven."[3]

Neither in the Hebrew Bible nor in the New Testament do we find such a focus on a dog, its breed, its color and size. Though the dog Qitmir appears in the Islamic version of the legend "The Seven Sleepers of Ephesus," no dog anywhere in the Bible is promised a place in heaven. The dog in the Qur'an does not appear in the chapter a second time, but its presence remains. Its pose of equanimity sets the tone for the events that follow, while it helps us to find balance in the turmoil of human activities: prejudice, religious persecution, and guile.

The fullness of the dog's loyalty or commitment can be understood only as counter to the merely intellectual acceptance of a doctrine. For this plenitude depends on a faith grounded in the reality of lived experience, as well as surrender to a heartening that solicits patience and endurance.

The sura of the Seven Sleepers is the only chapter of the Qur'an that "is read in the official reading of the Holy Writ every Friday in the mosques since the earliest times," writes Louis Massignon, a Catholic scholar who devoted his life to the study of Islam and was fascinated by the theme of the Seven Sleepers. He notes that the greatest Muslim historians and commentators over the centuries have been preoccupied by this legend, which "often influenced Muslim mentality, its symbolic art and its political eschatology."[4]

What is body? What is mind? How will the dead be raised? In what body will they come? Saint Paul in 2 Corinthians 12 indicates the kind of knowing that matters: "I knew a man in Christ above fourteen years ago, (whether in the body I cannot tell; or whether out of the body I cannot tell: God knoweth;) such an one caught up to the third heaven. And I knew such a man, (whether in the body, or out of the body, I cannot tell: God knoweth.)" Antinomies such as the dualism conjured in flesh and spirit are exceeded by the body itself, whether a physical body or a spiritual body.

The commentaries about "The People of the Cave" reflect on such familiar questions of life, death, and resurrection. God will rouse the sleepers, strengthening their hearts so that they can bear witness and denounce the polytheists in their midst. The long sleep of the youths and their waking after so many years, three full centuries, well past the time when they were in danger, was understood to be akin to the raising up of the dead into life everlasting. But, as I said, commentators reflect just as deeply on the nature of the dog. In the history of al-Tabari, we read the familiar refrain "God knows best how it happened." But in another, particularly absorbing story from the "Lives of the Prophets," as recounted by al-Thaʻlabi in the early eleventh century, we learn about the dog: what he looks like, how he acts, what he says. The dog is central to the revelation at hand, even though his ultimate fate remains unknown:

> When the youths saw the dog they said to one another that they were afraid that the dog would betray their presence by its barking, so they cursed him and drove him away with stones. When the dog saw them cursing him and driving him away with stones, he got up on his feet and walked proudly, saying in fluent, eloquent speech, "O people, do not drive me away, for

I bear witness that there is no god but Allah alone, Who has no partner. Let me protect you from your enemy and I will gain favor with God."

In an earlier account of the Prophet Mohammed's life by Ibn Ishaq, the dog remains with the youths. We are told more than once about him "stretching out his forelegs at the threshold of the door to the cave.[5]

I have long been drawn to the life of the spirit in the sinews of matter. The journey has taken me from fieldwork in Haiti to Locke's paraphrases of Saint Paul's epistles to the very real effects of case law on persons. Acknowledging my preoccupation throughout with metamorphosis or conversion, I knew that such transformation could be called sacred only because it fixated on what was unpalatable or irrational to the privileged and the powerful. An obsession with the body stays with me, along with Calvin's warning in his argument with Luther. Writing about transubstantiation in the *Institutes*, he admonishes Luther not to make Christ disappear under the "mask of the bread."

Though these compulsions rescued me, or at least promised some escape from the acceptable scripts of civility and propriety, I remained bound to a certain amount of discontent and gloom. It was only when dogs became part of my life that I learned to watch how they break through the barrier of reason and edge along the brink of faith.

Indebted to Eduardo Kohn's treatment of how we "live in worlds in which other selves [that] represent us can come to matter vitally," I am led to the cave, the dog at the threshold, and the humans inside. They are a powerful riposte to Plato's cave. There, we are given only the shadow of the ultimate *form* or idea, and we know ourselves benighted. How pernicious human idealism has been. It gives us reality only insofar as it relates to what lies beyond it.

So I chose a reality that finds the absolute in an entirely different register. In the mode of dogs, in their eyes and through their breath, taking the latter as indistinct from spirit or wind (Hebrew, *ruah*; Arabic, *ruh*), I stay alive in my body and my feelings. Of course, we can never attain the state of dogs. But to position oneself in this way, even if tenuously, both inside and outside a human background, is to let our bond with dogs count for something momentous. It puts us on the verge of what precedes judgment and escapes analysis or proof. Waiting, we stand steadfast at the entry of something unknown, apparently impossible, and utterly enchanting.

notes

By Way of Beginning

1. Jack Healy, "In Wyoming, Many Jobs, but No Place to Call Home," *New York Times*, January 12, 2013, http://www.nytimes.com/2013/01/13 /us/homelessness-increases-in-wyoming-product-of-economic-boom .html?pagewanted=all&_r=0 (accessed February 5, 2015).

2. Manny Fernandez, "Large Dogs in Public Housing Are Now Endangered Species," *New York Times*, September 22, 2009, http://www.nytimes .com/2009/09/23/nyregion/23dogs.html?module=Search&mabReward =relbias%3As (accessed February 5, 2015).

3. *Tracey v. Solesky*, 50 A.3d 1075, 427 Md. 627 (Md. 2012).

4. Ibid. (Greene, J., dissenting).

5. "Incoherent Definitions Confound Attempts to Label Dogs as 'Pit Bulls,'" *National Canine Research Council*, May 7, 2004, http://www .nationalcanineresearchcouncil.com/blog/incoherent-definitions-confound -attempts-to-label-dogs-as-pit-bulls/?doing_wp_cron=1399473188 .3006930351257324218750 (accessed February 5, 2015).

6. Dan Rodricks, "Pit Bulls: Own Them at Your Own Risk," *Baltimore Sun*, April 30, 2012, http://articles.baltimoresun.com/2012–04–30/news/bs-ed -rodricks-dogs-20120430_1_pit-bulls-towson-boy-dog-attacks (accessed February 5, 2015).

7. Quoted in Kate S. Alexander, "Maryland Shelters, Rescues Brace for Increase in Pit Bull Surrenders," Gazette.net, May, 4, 2012, http://www.gazette

.net/article/20120504/NEWS/705049659/1009/maryland-shelters-rescues-brace
-for-increase-in-pit-bull-surrenders&template=gazette (accessed February 5,
2015).

8. Kevin Rector, "Pit Bull Owners Say Neighborhood Ban Won't Make
Them Part with Dogs," *Baltimore Sun*, September 16, 2012, http://articles
.baltimoresun.com/2012–09–16/news/bs-md-pit-bull-owners-20120916_1
_pit-bull-armistead-homes-staffordshire-bull-terrier (accessed February 5,
2015); *Weigel v. Maryland*, 950 F. Supp.2d 811 (D. Md. 2013).

9. Arin Greenwood, "Maryland Does Right by Pit Bulls, Says They
Aren't Inherently Dangerous," *Huffington Post*, April 8, 2014, http://www
.huffingtonpost.com/2014/04/03/maryland-pit-bull-bill-_n_5086024.html
(accessed February 5, 2015).

10. "Man Sues City of Hawthorne, Calif. After Police Shoot, Kill His Dog,"
NewsOne, February 15, 2014, http://newsone.com/2890534/leon-rosby-man
-sues-city-of-hawthorne-calif-after-police-shoot-kill-kill-his-dog/ (accessed February 5, 2015); Leon Rosby has also started a Facebook page in memory of
Max, to raise funds for his defense and to fight for other dogs killed by police:
"OFFICIAL Page for Justice 4 Max about Max my Rottweiler who was killed
by the Hawthorne Police in Hawthorne, CA. Please visit 4 OFFICIAL latest/
breaking news & info. God Bless. Let's get Justice 4 Max and ALL DOGS
unjustly killed by police! by Leon Rosby."

11. Quoted in "Malcolm X: Make It Plain" (transcript), *The American
Experience*, season 6, episode 5, directed by Orlando Bagwell, aired January
26, 1994, www.pbs.org/wgbh/amex/malcolmx/filmmore/pt.html (accessed
February 5, 2015).

1. Dogs and Light

1. Vicki Hearne, *Tricks of the Light: New and Selected Poems* (Chicago:
University of Chicago Press, 2007), 10.

2. Hearne, "Tricks of the Light," in ibid., 89.

3. J. M. Coetzee, "The Philosophers and the Animals," in *The Lives of
Animals*, ed. Amy Gutman (Princeton, N.J.: Princeton University Press,
1999), 29.

4. Vicki Hearne, *Bandit: Dossier of a Dangerous Dog* (1991), republished as
Bandit: The Heart-Warming True Story of One Dog's Rescue from Death Row,
introduction by Elizabeth Marshall Thomas (New York: Skyhorse, 2007), 71.

5. Hearne, "Tricks of the Light," 85.

6. Peter Singer, *Animal Liberation*, new rev. ed. (New York: Avon Books,
1990), 2–21.

2. Back Talking Like I Did

1. W. B. Yeats, "A Poet to His Beloved," from *The Wind Among the Reeds*, in *The Poems: A New Edition*, ed. Richard J. Finneran (New York: Macmillan, 1983), 63.

2. Wallace Stevens, "No Possum, No Sop, No Taters," in *The Palm at the End of the Mind: Selected Poems and a Play*, ed. Holly Stevens (Hamden, Conn.: Archon Books, 1984), 247.

4. Dead Dogs

1. At all stages of the legal narrative, from the seizure to the charges to the actual photographs taken by the LA/SPCA, numbers vary. In my account of the number of dogs euthanized and the counts of dog fighting and animal cruelty, I follow "Gaming Enforcement Section Arrest Message," March 11, 2005, "Dogfighting (57 counts)"; "Cruelty to animals (57 counts)." The LA/SPCA announced that "68 fighting dogs" were taken into custody, with Boudreaux "facing up to 68 felony counts of owning, breeding, and fighting dogs" ("Legendary Dogfighter Detained," March 11, 2005). The Fifteenth Judicial District Court Application for Search Warrant by Jacob M. Dickinson (March 17, 2005) asserted that a search by "Gaming Agents" six days earlier "revealed 59 Pit Bull dogs." The "Notice Pending Forfeiture" on July 8, 2005, noted "57 counts of Dog Fighting, 59 counts of Animal Cruelty" (5). On November 14, 2005, Assistant District Attorney Ronald E. Dauterive informed Jason Robideaux, Boudreaux's lawyer, that his client was "arrested on 57 counts of dog fighting" and "57 counts of cruelty to animals." A count of the photographs of each dog taken for "evaluation" by the LA/SPCA comes to 49 dogs, but Floyd Boudreaux's list of his dogs adds up to 57.

2. The Humane Society has contributed a total of $800,000 to Louisiana State University, according to "HSUS Contributes Another $200,000 to LSU Shelter Medicine Program," October 1, 2011, dvm360, http://veterinarynews.dvm360.com/dvm/Veterinary+news/HSUS-delivers-another-200000-to-LSU-shelter-medici/ArticleStandard/Article/detail/742280 (accessed February 5, 2015).

3. Ruling on Constitutional Challenge of L.S.A.-R.S. 14:102.6(A)(1)(2), *Louisiana v. Boudreaux*, 2007-109393 (La. 6/28/07), 39 (quoting Tr. P. 22).

4. La. Rev. Stat. Ann. § 14: 102.6 A(2) (2012) (defining as contraband dogs seized in accordance with the state prohibition on dog fighting).

5. Judge Kristian Earles disposed of the case by granting the Boudreauxs' motion for acquittal. There was no published opinion.

6. *Louisiana v. Boudreaux*, 2007-109393 (La. 10/15/08), Trial Tr. Day 3:99–100.

7. The Louisiana Legislature has continued to amend the dog-fighting prohibition since its enactment in the animal cruelty statute, LSA-R.S.14.102, in 1982.

8. Floyd Boudreaux, interview, in Marc Joseph and James Frey, *American Pitbull* (Göttingen: Steidl, 2003), 48.

9. I first read about the Boudreaux dogs in "Pit Bull Breeder Floyd Boudreaux Acquitted of Dogfighting Charges," October 15, 2008, Blue Dog State, http://bluedogstate.blogspot.com/2008/10/pit-bull-breeder-floyd-boudreaux.html (accessed February 5, 2015). Other pit bull–loving sites that tell the story are "Louisiana v. Floyd Boudreaux," October 20, 2008, Staffy Lovin, http://lovinpitts.blogspot.com/2008/10/louisiana-v-floyd-boudreaux-who-are.html (accessed February 5, 2015); and "Interview with Legendary Dogman Floyd Boudreaux," Sporting Dog News, http://sportingdognews.blogspot.com/2013/05/floyd-boudreaux-interview.html (accessed February 5, 2015). For a video of Boudreaux's yard just two weeks before he was arrested, in which you can hear roosters crowing and Boudreaux talking about each of his dogs—which do flips and are healthy, well fed, and buoyant—see "F. Boudreaux Yard Video," April 27, 2011, YouTube, http://www.youtube.com/watch?v=IKDsw1O2zeM (accessed February 5, 2015). For photographs of the dogs, to the accompaniment of "Born on the Bayou," see "The Bulldogs of Boudreaux," January 26, 2012, YouTube, http://www.youtube.com/watch?v=T7eJmoCE1kA (accessed February 5, 2015).

10. J. W. Lambert Jr., Evangeline Veterinary Clinic, interview with author, Broussard, La., October 23, 2009.

11. Floyd Boudreaux, interview with author, Lafayette, La., October 23, 2009.

12. Louisiana SPCA, "Kathryn Destreza: Her Dedication to Protecting Animals Is 'Simply Amazing'" (press release), October 13, 2008, which has now been removed from http://www.la-spca.org/prevention/destreza.htm.

13. "ASPCA Names Regional Directors for Anti-Cruelty Initiatives," February 24, 2010, ASPCA, http://www.aspca.org/about-us/press-releases/aspca-names-regional-directors-anti-cruelty-initiatives (accessed February 5, 2015).

14. Quoted in "Internationally Known Pit-Pull Breeder Floyd Boudreaux and His Son Guy Are Charged with 48 Counts of Dog-Fighting and Possession of Steroids," *Daily Advertiser* (Lafayette, La.), March 23, 2005, http://www.zydecoonline.com/dev/index.php?name=News&file=print&sid=295 (accessed February 5, 2015).

15. Ibid.

16. Jason Robideaux, interview with author, Lafayette, La., October 22, 2009.

17. Jacob M. Dickinson, memorandum to Ronald E. Dauterive, lawyer for the LA/SPCA, August 21, 2006. See also Jacob M. Dickinson, testimony, *Louisiana v. Boudreaux*, Pre-Trial Hearing, October 16, 2006, 9, and Dickinson, Trial Tr. Day 3: 60.

18. Quoted in "Pit Bull Breeder Floyd Boudreaux Acquitted of Dogfighting Charges."

19. Floyd Boudreaux, interview with author, Lafayette, La., October 22, 2009.

20. Before the case proceeded to trial on the merits, the court first ruled on the defendants' motion to suppress evidence on the grounds that the seizure and destruction of the dogs violated the defendants' due process. The court denied their motion, and the evidence was ruled admissible. See Ruling on Constitutional Challenge of L.S.A.-R.S. 14:102.6(A)(1)(2), *Louisiana v. Boudreaux*, 2007–109393 (La. 6/28/07).

21. *Louisiana v. Boudreaux*, Trial Tr. Days 1–3, October 13–15, 2008. Quotations from the in-court examinations of Wendy Wolfson and Kathryn Destreza are taken from the trial transcript.

22. La. Rev. Stat. Ann. § 14: 102.6 A(2) (2012).

23. La. Rev. Stat. Ann. § 14: 102.5 B (2012) reads: "'Dogfighting' means an organized event wherein there is a display of combat between two or more dogs in which the fighting, killing, maiming, or injuring of a dog is the significant feature, or main purpose, of the event."

24. Jason Robideaux, cross-examination of Wendy Wolfson, *Louisiana v. Boudreaux*, Trial Tr. Day 2: 100–90; Day 3: 3–24. The photographs are taken from the state's exhibit. Each document consists of one, two, or three pages of pictures followed by a single evaluation sheet.

25. *Louisiana v. Boudreaux*, Trial Tr. Day 3: 97–98. Cockfighting became illegal in Louisiana only in 2011, three years later. See La. Rev. Stat. Ann. § 14: 102.23 (2012).

26. Jason Robideaux, cross-examination of Kathryn Destreza, *Louisiana v. Boudreaux*, Trial Tr. Day 3: 30–43.

27. Quoted in Mike Perlstein, "Fighting Back," *New Orleans Times-Picayune*, May 9, 2005.

28. *Louisiana v. Boudreaux*, Trial Tr. Day 3:102–3.

29. Criminal Code, La. Rev. Stat. 14:102.6; 14:102.6(A)(2); 14:102.7; 14:102.5(A)7(b)(iii).

30. Affidavit for Warrant of Arrest, Fifteenth Judicial Dist. Ct., Parish of Lafayette, State of Louisiana, Case #CGD050127, sworn to and signed by Jacob M. Dickinson, March, 11, 2005; Initial Complaint/Offense Report, Louisiana Dep't of Public Safety and Corrections, Office of State Police, Bureau of Investigations, received by Jacob M. Dickinson, 01-24-05 (Date of Complaint) and 03-11-05 (Date of Offense); Jacob Dickinson, testimony, *Louisiana v. Boudreaux*, Trial Tr. Day 2: 27ff.

31. Jacob Dickinson, testimony, *Louisiana v. Boudreaux*, Trial Tr. Day 2: 29–30.

32. *Sentell v. New Orleans and C.R. Co.*, 166 U.S. 698 (1897). In ruling on the constitutionality of the Louisiana dog-fighting statute in *Louisiana v. Boudreaux*, Judge Marilyn C. Castle relied on *Sentell v. New Orleans and C.R. Co.* See Ruling on Constitutional Challenge of L.S.A.-R.S. 14:102.6(A)(1)(2), *Louisiana v. Boudreaux*, 2007-109393 (La. 6/28/07), 40.

33. Boudreaux interview, October 23, 2009.

34. Vicki Hearne, *Adam's Task: Calling Animals by Name* (New York: Harper Perennial, 1994), x.

35. David Harry Stewart, "Rescued Fighting Dogs Await Adoption," *Time*, November 28, 2009 (for a video, see http://content.time.com/time/video /player/0,32068,52925818001_1943278,00.html [accessed February 5, 2015]). See also David von Drehle, "Can Attack Dogs Be Rehabilitated?" *Time*, December 7, 2009.

5. Speaking About Extinction

1. *Carter v. Dow*, 16 Wis. 298 (Wis. 1862).

2. For a video of the Bolio and Tombstone dogs, see "Pat Patrick Yard, 1996," July 26, 2013, YouTube, https://www.youtube.com/watch?v=P80_60YF1QA #aid=P-CVS4XMHag (accessed February 5, 2015).

3. Despite the acquittals of Patrick and Dennis, a Pima County Superior Court judge later ordered the forfeiture of the property where Dennis had bred and sold dogs. See Kim Smith, "Woman Must Forfeit Property: Judge: Felonies Were Committed in Selling, Breeding Dogs to Fight," *Arizona Daily Star* (Tucson), April 7, 2010, http://tucson.com/news/local/crime /article_26658120-3cf4-5535-bbd1-573d7a500021.html (accessed February 5, 2015).

4. "Dogfighting Takes Another Huge Hit: Pat Patrick Goes Down," Democratic Underground, http://www.democraticunderground.com/discuss /duboard.php?az=view_all&address=231x17756 (accessed February 5, 2015).

5. A powerful account of the greed and cruelty of Pima County law enforcement in cahoots with the Humane Society is "HSUS Dogfight Czar John Goodwin Fails Again," November 29, 2008, Blue Dog State, http:// bluedogstate.blogspot.com/2008/11/hsus-dogfight-czar-john-goodwin-fails. html (accessed February 5, 2015).

6. Pima County Attorney's Office, "Major Victory for County Attorney's Office in Animal Abuse Case" (press release), April 6, 2010, http://www.pcao .pima.gov/documents/AssetForfeitureOfOrangeGroveAnimalAbuseCase.pdf (accessed February 5, 2015).

7. There is some precedent for seizing property as a deterrent to dog fighting. See, for example, Humane Society, "The HSUS Helps Kalamazoo County Seize 46 Dogs," August 6, 2012, http://www.humanesociety.org/news /press_releases/2012/08/michigan_dogfight_raid_080612.html#id=album -153&num=content-2881 (accessed February 5, 2105). The ASPCA claims that 25 percent of dog-fighting cases result in the seizure of assets, including real property, in "Prosecutor's Guide to Dogfighting Cases," 2010, New England Animal Control/Humane Academy, http://www.neacha.org/resources /prosecutors.dogfight.pdf (accessed February 5, 2105).

8. Pima County Attorney's Office, "Major Victory for County Attorney's Office in Animal Abuse Case."

9. Monte Mitchell, "Pit Bulls Destroyed," *Winston-Salem Journal*, December 12, 2012.

10. "Cajun Rules," Sporting Dog, http://www.sporting-dog.com/select -pages/cajunrules.html (accessed February 6, 2015). Early accounts of the vanished era of dog fighting and the champion dogs that lived for the fight are George C. Armitage, *Thirty Years with Fighting Dogs* (Washington, D.C.: Jack Jones, 1935); and Richard K. Fox, *The Dog Pit: Or, How to Select, Breed, Train, and Manage Fighting Dogs, with Points as to Their Care in Health and Disease* (1888; repr., Cookhill, Alcester: Read Country Books, 2005). In *Pick-A-Winna: A Pit Bull Documentary* [booklet accompanying a video], Robert Stevens also recounts the "complete fight game" as it existed in the 1970s.

11. Richard F. Stratton, *The World of the American Pit Bull Terrier* (Neptune, N.J.: TFH, 1983), 205, 241–45. Like so much else that has to do with these dogs, the books about them garner praise and revulsion, as do the writers—Stratton and even Vicki Hearne—depending on whom you read. Two of the now numerous arguments against Stratton and his ilk are "Richard Stratton Is A," May 24, 2006, The Happy Pit Bull, http://happypitbull.blogspot.com/2006/05 /richard-stratton-is-criminal.html (accessed February 6, 2015); and Dianne Jessup, "Dog Fighting: The Truth," WorkingPitBull, http://www.workingpitbull .com/dogfighting2.htm (accessed February 6, 2015). Other vehement and distorted attacks appear at "Summer Reading List: II," August 21, 2014, Sudden, Random, Unprovoked & Violent: Pit Bulls in a Humane Society, http:// sruv-pitbulls.blogspot.com/2014/08/summer-reading-list-ii.html (accessed February 6, 2015); and "Essential Reading," Sudden, Random, Unprovoked & Violent: Pit Bulls in a Humane Society, http://sruv-pitbulls.blogspot.com/p /essential-reading.html (accessed April 8, 2014). Blogs against the breed of men and dogs include The Truth About Pit Bulls, http://thetruthaboutpitbulls .blogspot.com/2010/10/americas-dog-tige.html; DogsBite: Some Dogs Don't Let Go, http://www.dogsbite.org; Craven Desires, http://cravendesires.blogspot .com; and 17 Barks: Musings on Canidae and Alternative Views of Life, http://17barks.blogspot.com (all accessed February 6, 2015).

6. Fable for the End of a Breed

1. *United States v. Stevens*, No. 2:04-cr-0051-ANB (W.D. Pa., November 10, 2004), vacated by 559 U.S. 460 (2010), 18 U.S.C.§ 48, also known as the Depiction of Animal Cruelty Act. The Supreme Court later held that the statute was constitutionally overbroad and thus abridged Stevens's right to free speech.

2. Bob Stevens, *Dogs of Velvet and Steel: Pit Bulldogs: A Manual for Owners* (Charlotte, N.C.: Herb Eaton Historical Publications; Marceline, Mo: Walsworth, 1983), was marketed by Amazon, Borders, and Barnes & Noble. When I began writing about Stevens, I tried to order his book on Amazon. Though it was advertised for $500 and up, it was impossible to find a copy. My library found it at the Library of Congress, but when I ordered it on interlibrary loan, it turned out not to be on the shelves. Stevens published a revised edition—*Dogs of Velvet and Steel: Pit Bulldogs: A Manual for Owners, the Epilogue* (Altavista, Va.: Pine Haven, 2012), prefaced with nearly two hundred new pages about his seven-year struggle in the courts and the story behind his life's work (writing about and living with the American pit bull terrier)—as well as an account of his faith in Christ and his will to believe. That dedication to a life of grace in the Lord is displayed on his Web site, created after the Supreme Court decision and his "victory," http://www.pitbullvictory.com (accessed February 6, 2015). In my notes, part 1 refers to the later volume and part 2 to the earlier one, since that is how they are published.

3. Stevens, *Dogs of Velvet and Steel*, rev. ed., part 2, 629, 191.

4. Robert Stevens, *Pick-A-Winna: A Pit Bull Documentary* [booklet accompanying the video], 14, sent to author by mail, January 25, 2014.

5. Buchanan has since become a partner in the New York office of a global law firm. Radley Balko, "Mary Beth Buchanan Finally Quits; Regrets Not Having Been Even Douchier," November 19, 2009, Reason.com: Free Minds and Free Markets, http://reason.com/blog/2009/11/19/mary-beth-buchanan -finally-qui (accessed February 6, 2015).

6. *United States v. Stevens*, 533 F.3d, 218, 220–21 (3d Cir. 2008) (en banc).

7. *United States v. Stevens*, 559 U.S. 460 (2010).

8. On April 21, 2010, one day after the Supreme Court struck down in the *Stevens* case the federal law banning the creation, sale, and possession of materials depicting acts of animal cruelty, its original sponsor, Representative Elton Gallegly (R-Calif.), introduced H.R. 5092, a bill with much more specific language intended to apply only to "crush videos." It prohibits selling or offering for sale any depictions of animals being crushed, drowned, impaled, or burned where such actions are illegal. On December 9, 2010, President Barack Obama signed into law H.R. 5566, the Animal Crush Video Prohibition Act of 2010 (Pub. L. No. 111-294, 124 Stat. 3177, *amending* 18 U.S.C. § 48).

9. Stevens, *Dogs of Velvet and Steel*, rev. ed., part 2, 629–30.

10. Wayne Pacelle, "Animal Rights and Speech" [letter to the editor], *New York Times*, September 25, 2009.

11. *United States v. Stevens*, 559 U.S. at 470.

12. Brief for Respondent, 18–27, *United States v. Stevens*, 559 U.S. 460.

13. I. Lehr Brisbin, District Court testimony, quoted in ibid., 6–7.

14. *United States v. Stevens*, 533 F.3d at 218, 221.

15. Brief for Respondent, 11, *United States v. Stevens*, 559 U.S. 460.

16. Ibid., 57.

17. Brief for the DKT Liberty Project, American Civil Liberties Union, and Center for Democracy and Technology et al. as Amici Curiae in Support of Respondent, *United States v. Stevens*, 559 U.S. 460.

18. Brief for Constitutional Law Scholars Bruce Ackerman et al. as Amici Curiae in Support of Respondent, *United States v. Stevens*, 559 U.S. 460.

19. Brief for Respondent, 50, *United States v. Stevens*, 559 U.S. 460.

20. Bob Stevens, letter to author, May 25, 2013. Since Robert Stevens publishes under and corresponds using the name Bob, I refer to him in that way.

21. Humane Society, "Who Is Bob Stevens? Focus of *United States v. Stevens*," November 9, 2009, http://www.humanesociety.org/news/news/2009/11/bob_stevens_110909.html; and "Frequently Asked Questions About Bob Stevens: First Conviction Under the Animal Cruelty Depictions Act," November 9, 2009, http://www.humanesociety.org/news/news/2009/11/faq_bob_stevens_110909.html#.UoVeJV5jp94 (both accessed February 6, 2015).

22. The government witnesses, in order of their appearance, were Timothy C. Knapp, state trooper, Commonwealth of Pennsylvania; Raymond Quijas, U.S. postal inspector and former special agent with the Drug Enforcement Administration; Mark Thomas Kumpf, superintendent of animal services for the city of Newport, Virginia; and Dr. Harvey Bendix, hospital director and owner of the Norwin Veterinary Hospital in North Huntington, Pennsylvania.

23. Bob Stevens, letter to author, August 9, 2012.

24. Bob Stevens, CV, sent to author, June 17, 2013.

25. Stevens, *Dogs of Velvet and Steel*, rev. ed., part 2, 193. The boxer Francisco Antonio Rodriguez Brito—called "Morochito"—was actually Venezuelan.

26. Ibid., 300.

27. Bob Stevens, letter to author, April 10, 2014.

28. Bob Stevens, letter to author, March 30, 2014.

29. Stevens, *Pick-A-Winna*, 6.

30. Stevens, *Dogs of Velvet and Steel*, rev. ed., part 2, 432.

31. "The Best Game of All," included in Bob Stevens, letter to author, April 23, 2013.

32. Bob Stevens, letter to author, March 14, 2013.

33. Stevens, *Dogs of Velvet and Steel*, rev. ed., part 1, 107.

34. Stevens, "Best Game of All."

35. Ibid.

36. Ibid.

37. Preface to *Pit Pro* [forthcoming], included in Bob Stevens, letter to author, November 7, 2013; and "Let's Talk Dogs," July 4, 2010, PitBullVictory, http://www.pitbullvictory.com/Articles_Updates.html (accessed February 6, 2015).

38. Stevens, *Dogs of Velvet and Steel*, rev. ed., part 2, 258, 259–60.

39. Stevens, "Let's Talk Dogs."

40. Stevens, preface to *Pit Pro.*

41. *United States v. Stevens*, 533 F.3d 218, 221, Transcript of Jury Trial Proceedings on Wednesday, January 12, 2005, in the United States District Court for the Western District of Pennsylvania, before Alan N. Block, Senior District Court Judge, 54. I thank Bob Stevens for sending me a copy of this transcript on January 25, 2014.

42. Robert Stevens, "Information Regarding Your Movie 'Catch Dogs,'" 3, sent to author by mail, January 2014.

43. *Baze v. Rees*, 553 U.S. 35 (2008).

44. Bob Stevens, letter to author, April 11, 2014.

45. Stevens, "Best Game of All."

46. Bob Stevens, letters to author, June 6 and August 9, 2012.

47. Stevens, *Dogs of Velvet and Steel*, rev. ed., part 2, 192.

48. Ibid., part 1, 19.

49. Ibid., 25.

50. Ibid., 22.

Part III. Pariah Dogs

1. "Suffering Dogs: The Canine Exiles from Constantinople," *Advertiser* (Adelaide, Australia), October 3, 1910.

2. Sam Cooper and Sean Sullivan, "Massacre Horrifies B.C.: Man Shoots 100 Sled Dogs 'Execution-Style' After Olympic Showdown," *Province* (Vancouver), February 6, 2011, http://www.theprovince.com/life/Massacre+horrifies+shoots+sled+dogs+execution+style+after+Olympic+slowdown/4197145/story.html (accessed February 6, 2015). Other reports mention fifty-six or even as few as fifty-two dogs: Eric Mackenzie, "SPCA Removes 56 Bodies from Sled Dog Grave," *Question* (Whistler, B.C.), May 12, 2011, http://www.whistlerquestion.com/spca-removes-56-bodies-from-sled-dog-grave-1.1288792; and "52 Whistler Sled Dogs Exhumed: B.C. SPCA," CBC News (British Columbia), May 8, 2011, http://www.cbc.ca/news/canada/british-columbia/52-whistler-sled-dogs-exhumed-b-c-spca-1.1032491 (both accessed May 19, 2015).

3. Associated Press, "Dogs Found Shot in Head at South Carolina Landfill, Animal Control Officers Accused," *Huffington Post*, March 7, 2011, http://www.huffingtonpost.com/2011/03/07/dogs-shot-in-head-south -carolina_n_832365.html (accessed February 6, 2015).

4. Quoted in Ruby Russell, "Bucharest's Looming Dog Slaughter," *Global Post*, May 1, 2011, http://www.globalpost.com/dispatch/news/regions/europe /110429/bucharest-romania-stray-dogs (accessed February 6, 2015).

5. Kirit Radia, "Sochi Culling Stray Dogs Ahead of the Olympics," January 31, 2014, ABC News, http://abcnews.go.com/blogs/headlines/2014/01/sochi-culling-stray-dogs-ahead-of-the-olympics/ (accessed February 6, 2015).

6. Malcolm Lowry, *Under the Volcano* (1947; New York: HarperCollins, 2000), 388.

7. J. M. Coetzee, *Disgrace* (New York: Penguin, 1999), 146, 205.

8. William Carlos Williams, *Paterson*, ed. Christopher MacGowan (New York: New Directions, 1992), 3, 61, 103.

9. Ibid., 44, 53, 65, 7, 79.

10. Ibid., 57.

11. Ibid., 131.

7. Through the Eyes of Dogs

1. Jean-Luc Godard, "Synopsis," Festival de Cannes, http://www.festival -cannes.com/en/archives/ficheFilm/id/100011773/year/2014.html (accessed February 6, 2015). The film won the Jury Prize at Cannes.

2. Quoted in "Nouvelle Wag: 'White God' Wins Cannes' Palm Dog," May 23, 2014, Aol.com, http://www.aol.com/article/2014/05/23/nouvelle-wag -white-god-wins-cannes-palm-dog/20891509/ (accessed February 6, 2015).

3. Andrea Luka Zimmerman's next film, the award-winning *Estate, a Reverie*, premiered in London on November 21, 2014, after taking seven years to make. An intensely collaborative project, this "documentary essay" captures the sense of community that was destroyed when the housing project Samuel House—the final block in Hackney's Haggerston estate—was demolished to make way for a luxury apartment complex. The background and reach of Zimmerman's film-making can be found at "Estate, a Reverie," Fugitive Images, http://www.fugitiveimages.org.uk/projects/estatefilm/; and "Estate: A Reverie," http://www.estatefilm.co.uk/ (both accessed February 6, 2015).

4. Andrea Luka Zimmerman, "On Common Ground: The Making of Meaning in Film and Life," October 3, 2013, open Democracy: free thinking for the world, http://www.opendemocracy.net/print/75783 (accessed February 6, 2015). See also "Andrea Luka Zimmerman's CV," Fugitive Images, http://www.fugitiveimages.org.uk/andrea-cv (accessed February 6, 2015).

5. Sara Gates, "Dogs Teargassed in Turkey by Police During Protests," *Huffington Post*, June 6, 2013, http://www.huffingtonpost.com/2013/06/06 /dogs-teargassed-in-turkey_n_3397027.html (accessed February 6, 2015). Andrea Luka Zimmerman, e-mail to author, June 29, 2014.

6. Andrea Luka Zimmerman, "Come Together: The Making of Meaning in Film and Life, a Manifest of a Film Maker," *Interference: International Journal of Film and Festival Reviews*, http://www.xxxinterferencexxx.com /essays_2013_Zimmerman_Taskafa.html (accessed February 6, 2015).

7. Gülen Güler, e-mail to author, June 30, 2014.

8. Eduardo Kohn, *How Forests Think: Toward an Anthropology Beyond the Human* (Berkeley: University of California Press, 2013), 14. This book elaborates on Kohn's groundbreaking article on a radically generative "ecology of selves": "How Dogs Dream: Amazonian Natures and the Politics of Transspecies Engagement," *American Ethnologist* 34, no. 1 (2007): 3–24.

9. Zimmerman, "On Common Ground."

10. John Berger, *King: A Street Story* (1999; New York: Vintage, 2000).

11. Ibid., 5.

12. Serge Avedikian calls it Oxia, which, like Sivri in Turkish, means "sharp" in Greek. This island in the Sea of Marmara is little more than a rock, and a little farther out than the other islands. It is also called Hayırsızada, which actually means "no good" or "worthless."

13. Zimmerman, "On Common Ground."

14. Andrea Luka Zimmerman, e-mail to author, October 27, 2013.

15. Berger, *King*, 7, 146.

16. Quoted in Alexander Christie-Miller, "Istanbul Residents Rally Around Their Beloved Stray Dogs," *Christian Science Monitor*, October 31, 2012, http://www.csmonitor.com/World/Middle-East/2012/1031/Istanbul -residents-rally-around-their-beloved-stray-dogs (accessed February 9, 2015).

17. Dalia Mortada, "Istanbul's Forgotten Dogs Struggle for Survival," *DW*, August 10, 2013, http://www.dw.de/istanbuls-forgotten-dogs-struggle -for-survival/a-16997550 (accessed February 9, 2015); Kristina Chew, "Turkey's Solution for Stray Dogs Is to Send Them Far Away, Where They Can't Survive," October 19, 2013, care2, http://www.care2.com/causes/turkeys -solution-for-stray-dogs-is-to-send-them-far-away-where-they-cant-survive. html (accessed February 9, 2015). Although the government withdrew this controversial amendment to its animal protection law 1599, the draft legislation is now on the table again.

18. Orhan Pamuk, *My Name Is Red*, trans. Erdağ M. Göknar (New York: Knopf, 2001), 12.

19. Mark Twain, *The Innocents Abroad or, The New Pilgrims' Progress*, intro. Jane Jacobs (New York: Modern Library, 2003), 268, 268, 269.

20. Annika Eriksson, *I am the dog that was always here (loop)*, was commissioned for KIOSKgallery, Ghent, and the thirteenth Istanbul Biennial in 2013, http://vimeo.com/68115849 (accessed February 9, 2015).

8. If I Sense the Beauty

1. Written and directed by Peter Brosens and Dorjkhandyn Turmunkh, *State of Dogs* (1998) is the second film in the *Mongolia Trilogy*, which includes *City of the Steppes* (1993) and *Poets of Mongolia* (1999).

2. According to the film's press materials, the film so deeply affected Damchaa that "the famous 'voice of Mongolia' told journalists [from the *Mongol Messenger*] that he could now happily die, having produced his finest possible work."

3. Peter Brosens worked as a cultural anthropologist in Ecuador, where he filmed his first documentaries. Dorjkhandyn Turmunkh is a journalist and program director with Mongolian National Broadcaster, the state-funded television channel, as well as a scriptwriter, producer, and founder of the independent production company Tobch Toli Productions. He wrote and produced the feature film *Tears of Lama* (1992). Since its release in 1998, *State of Dogs* has won seventeen international awards.

4. Reviews of *State of Dogs* include Leah Kohlenberg, "Die Like a Dog," *Time*, January 25, 1999, http://content.time.com/time/world/article /0,8599,2054104,00.html; Fukushima Yukio, *State of Dogs*, YIDFF 1999, http://www.yidff.jp/99/cato49/99c058-2-e.html; Bhob Stewart, *State of Dogs* [review summary], *New York Times*, http://www.nytimes.com/movies/movie /173775/State-of-Dogs/overview; and David Dalgleish, "*Nohoi Oron: State of Dogs*," Full Alert Film Review, http://wlt4.home.mindspring.com/fafr /reviews/state.htm (all accessed February 9, 2015). See also Michaela Schäuble, "The Ethnographer's Eye: Vision, Narration, and Poetic Imagery in Contemporary Anthropological Film," in *Writing and Seeing: Essays on Word and Image*, ed. Rui Carvalho Homem and Maria de Fátima Lambert (Amsterdam: Rodopi, 2006), 301–12.

5. Peter Brosens, e-mail to author, August 1, 2014.

Coda

1. *The Koran Interpreted: A Translation*, trans. A. J. Arberry (1955; London: Oxford University Press, 1964), sura 18:22–26.

2. Kenneth Burke, *The Rhetoric of Religion: Studies in Logology* (1961; Berkeley: University of California Press, 1970), 21.

3. *'Arā'is al-majālis fī qiṣaṣ al-anbiyā'* or *"Lives of the Prophets,"* as Recounted by Abū Isḥāq Aḥmad ibn Muḥammad ibn Ibrāhīm al-Thaʿlabī (1035), trans. and anno. William M. Brinner (Leiden: Brill, 2002), 696–97.

4. "Discourse by Professor L. Massignon at the International Congress at Brussels on the 5th of September, 1939," trans. F. Krenkow, *Islamic Culture* 15 (1941): 267–70.

5. *'Arā'is al-majālis fī qiṣaṣ al-anbiyā'*, 705–6.

acknowledgments

THIS BOOK BEGAN WITH THE KILLING of dogs, the American pit bull terriers of Floyd Boudreaux. Not long after reading about their seizure and quick dispatch by the Louisiana ASPCA, I traveled to Lafayette, Louisiana. The hours I spent with Jason Robideaux, Boudreaux's first lawyer, at the Lafayette District (Parish) Courthouse determined the course of my work. Not only did he provide me with court transcripts, testimonies, and evidence used in court—most important, copies of the photos and evaluations of Boudreaux's dogs—but his courage renewed my faith in the capacity of law, in the right hands, to challenge the prosecutorial and discriminatory practices of the state.

Floyd Boudreaux, his voice, steadfastness, and faith remain with me still. Though we spent only one evening and the better part of a day together, he impressed me deeply. Not only his dedication to the memory of the dogs he had bred and loved for so long but also his capacity for forgiveness, his strength in spite of devastating loss. That loss so inconceivable to me at the time became understandable when I learned more about a different kind of attachment, what Harlan Weaver calls "a funny kind of love," between men and their dogs.

Above all, there is Bob Stevens, who has both reminded me and taught me, in our correspondence and through his lifelong writing about the breed—his "dogs of velvet and steel"—that nobility and commitment can never be compromised. Not by the state, the courts, or the disciplinary power of humane organizations. Not if you hold fast to your beliefs and stay honest with yourself and others. Stevens taught me more about the life of the spirit, about dogs and training, generosity and perseverance, than anyone I have ever known.

Though I never took that drive to his home in the hills of Virginia, I count him as a friend and teacher. His letters, written with grace and wit, kept me going in difficult times. Bob's sensitivity and concern for the animals in his life—both human and nonhuman—capture what it means to dwell in that space where profoundly difficult conversations matter, where writing itself is inseparable from the quest for justice. If this book comes close to the ideal I had in mind when I began, I owe it to him.

Writing this book also brought into my life four artists whose work motivated its final section, "Pariah Dogs." Serge Avedikian's stunning *Barking Island* introduced me to the stray dogs of Istanbul. I am grateful to Avedikian, the director; Ron Dyens, the producer; and the artist Thomas Azuélos for the use of the image that graces the cover of this book. Peter Brosens encouraged me greatly. His *Mongolia Trilogy*, especially *State of Dogs*, gave visionary heft to these pages. Annika Eriksson's video loop *I am the dog that was always here* challenged me to come to terms with the meaning of abandonment. Andrea Luka Zimmerman, an activist, writer, and filmmaker of tremendous force, inspired me throughout this project. My ongoing debt to her—and the film *Taşkafa*—is too extensive to be adequately acknowledged here. Let me just say how grateful I am not only for her brilliant documentary films but also for her words, their audacity and prescience. I thank them all for their support of my project and for the permission they granted me to use stills from their films here.

I am keenly aware of my debt to the dog people and others with creaturely sensibilities in my midst for whom I write and with whom I think. They give me courage and calm: Sharon Cameron, Carla Freccero, Donna Haraway, Lori Gruen, Susan McHugh, Anat Pick, Deborah Rose, Harlan Weaver.

Friends, here in Nashville and elsewhere, have incited, inspired, and challenged me in numerous ways. For their involvement with and conversations about dogs, and the path this book would track, I thank Thomas Campbell, Max Cavitch, David Clark, Jennifer Fay, Denis Flannery, Andrew Krichels, David Lloyd, Kelly Oliver, and David Wood. Avery Gordon, ever a muse, told me I should see the film *Taşkafa*. To the women of Nashville Pittie—Pit Bull Initiative to Transform Image and Educate—I give thanks for their efforts to rescue and reclaim the lives of dogs: Carlene Castleman, Jana Mandes, and Jen Kilgore, along with her miraculous American pit bull terrier Flat Stouie. I also thank Jamie C. Adams and Bill Brimm for their assistance with the book's photos. Carolyn Dever, then Dean of Arts and Sciences at Vanderbilt, provided invaluable support.

Twenty-seven years ago in a book on Poe, I first acknowledged my debt to Ronald Paulson. Since then, he has been my most arduous reader and critic. Tough and quick and brilliant, there is no one quite like him.

A number of individuals worked closely with me during various stages of this project. I thank Patricia Ann Millett, now judge of the United States

Court of Appeals for the District of Columbia Circuit, who assisted me in making the initial contact with Bob Stevens. Faith Barter's comments were useful throughout, and her help was crucial to the section "When Law Comes to Visit." Thanks also go to Petal Samuel, Sarah Clark, and Simon Waxman, who commented on the final version.

Wendy Lochner, my editor at Columbia University Press, nurtured this book with her great insights and inspiring presence. Her enthusiasm and serene brilliance made its completion possible. To the editorial expertise and constancy of Christine Dunbar, I owe an immense debt of gratitude. I am also indebted to Irene Pavitt for her guidance during the final stages of production.

Parts of "By Way of Beginning" were published in an earlier form in Colin Dayan, "Short Cuts," *London Review of Books*, December 3, 2009, 24; parts of "Dead Dogs" were published in an earlier form in "Dead Dogs," *Boston Review*, March 1, 2010; and parts of "Pariah Dogs" were published in an earlier form in "Like a Dog," *Boston Review*, July 1, 2011. I thank John Sturrock and Deb Chasman for the opportunity to publish these earlier articles and for permission to reprint here.

My husband, David Wasserstein, remains a lodestone in this world of inconstancy, a goad to inquiry, sometimes conflicting but always galvanizing, as these pages bear out.

This book is dedicated to the memory of Mehdi, the dog whose presence abides in the body and spirit of Stella, who shares that space of recognition with him.

permissions

"Book I" (fourteen-line excerpt) by William Carlos Williams, from *Paterson*, copyright © 1946 by William Carlos Williams. Reprinted by permission of New Directions Publishing Corp.

"Book II" (excerpts totaling nine lines) by William Carlos Williams, from *Paterson*, copyright © 1948 by William Carlos Williams. Reprinted by permission of New Directions Publishing Corp.

"Book III" (sixteen-line excerpt) by William Carlos Williams, from *Paterson*, copyright © 1949 by William Carlos Williams. Reprinted by permission of New Directions Publishing Corp.

Eric Fried, "Definition," from *Warngedichte* (*Warning Poems*, 1964). Reprinted with permission of Carl Hanser Verlag.

Film stills from *I Am the Dog That Was Always Here (loop)* are reproduced courtesy of Annika Eriksson, Krome Gallery, and Galeri NON.

Film stills from *Taşkafa* are reproduced courtesy of Andrea Luka Zimmerman.

Film stills from *State of Dogs* are reproduced courtesy of Brosens-Woodworth.

Frame from Serge Avedikian, *Barking Island* is reproduced courtesy of Serge Avedikian, Ron Dyens, and Thomas Azuélos.

"Rembrandt" (six-line poetic fragment) by W. G. Sebald, translated by Michael Hamburger, from *Unrecounted*, copyright © 2004 by The Estate of W. G. Sebald, translation © 2004 by Michael Hamburger. Reprinted by permission of New Directions Publishing Corp.

"Rembrandt" (six-line poetic fragment) by W. G. Sebald, translated by Michael Hamburger, from *Unrecounted*, copyright © 2004 by The Estate of W. G. Sebald, translation © 2004 by Michael Hamburger. Reprinted by permission of Penguin Books Ltd.

Tricks of the Light: New and Selected Poems by Vicki Hearne; edited with an introduction by John Hollander. © 2007 University of Chicago Press. Reprinted by permission.

index

116, 123–25, 128–29, 132, 134–35,
141, 142; thoughts of, 10, 28–29;
through the eyes of, 121–40;
"weapon," 101. *See also* catch dogs;
dog breeds; dog fighting
Douglass, Frederick, 21
Duffaut, Préfête, 48
Dylan, Bob, *The Freewheelin' Bob Dylan*, 33

Earles, Kristian, 54, 70–71
Eco (dog in Istanbul), 129
Edwards, Jonathan, 10
Elijah Muhammad, 33
Eliot, T. S., "Burnt Norton," 150
Eriksson, Annika, *I am the dog that was always here (loop)*, 136–40
Ewing, John, *Hood Dawgs*, 90

Fanon, Frantz, xiv
Faron, Ed, 76, 80–81
Firmin, Geoffrey (character in *Under the Volcano*), 116
First Amendment rights, 87, 89–90, 91, 93, 97
Fried, Erich, "Definition," 141
Fuller, Samuel, *White Dog*, 9, 122

Gabbey, Aileen, 6
gameness, in dogs, 103–4
Gary, Romain, *White Dog*, 9
Giuliani, Rudolph, 4
Gnadentod (mercy killing; death by grace), 76
Godard, Jean-Luc, *Goodbye to Language*, 121–22
Goodwin, John, 78
Greene, Clayton, 5
Güler, Gülen, 124

Haasar (dog in Mongolian legend), 153

Haiti, dogs in, 49–50
Hammonds, Gary, 109
Haraway, Donna, 11
Hawthorne Police Department (California), 7–8
Hearne, Vicki, 17–22, 75, 110; dogs of (Annie and Michael), 18
WRITINGS OF: *Adam's Task: Calling Animals by Name*, 75; *Bandit: Dossier of a Dangerous Dog*, 19–20; "News from the Dogs," 17; "Tricks of the Light," 17, 20
Henry, Matthew, *Commentary on the Whole Bible*, 27–28
Holy Trinity Cathedral (Haiti), 48
humane organizations, collusion of with police, 76
Humane Society of the United States (HSUS), 6, 53, 54, 56, 57, 58, 75, 76, 78, 79, 81, 88, 89, 91, 92, 96, 97, 103
humane treatment: abstract concern with, 93–94; claims of, 19; pretense of, 75–76, 89

Ibn Ishaq, 161
Istanbul, dogs in, 123–36

Jesse (author's dog), 18, 23, 24, 29, 37–38, 44
Johnny (author's family's dog), 32, 44
Jones, Ashton, 33

Katyal, Neal, 90
Keeler, Christine, 33
Kennedy, John F., 32–33
King (canine character in *King: A Street Story*), 130, 131
King, Martin Luther, Jr., 32
Kohn, Eduardo, *How Forests Think: Toward an Anthropology Beyond the Human*, 124, 161

for dog fighting, criminality, and mauling of children, 87; seizures, detentions, and exterminations of, xv, 53–54, 57–58, 71–74, 75–76, 81–82. *See also* American pit bull terriers; American Staffordshire terriers; Mehdi; Stella

Plato, 161

police: collusion of, with humane organizations, 76; and humane law enforcement, 56–57, 67, 88; power of, 71–72

positive reinforcement (of dogs), cautions with, 19

Qitmir (dog in Islamic legend), 159

Qur'an, dog story from, 157–61

racial profiling, 8

racism, 2, 3, 121, 122

Roberts, John, 107

Robideaux, Jason (J Robi), 54, 55, 57, 62, 63, 64, 66, 67, 68, 69, 70, 83

Rodricks, Dan, 6

Roma, David, *Off the Chain*, 90

Rosby, Leon, 7–8, 9; dog of (Max), 7–9

Roxy Miéville (canine character in *Goodbye to Language*), 122

Sayres, Ed, 57

Sebald, W. G., "Rembrandt," 121

Sentell v. New Orleans and C. R. Co. (1897), 73–74

Sergeant Stubby (military dog), 88

"Seven Sleepers of Ephesus, The," 159–60

Shannon, Dan, 75

Singer, Peter, 20, 21

Sotomayor, Sonia, 90

spirit: life of, and thought of dogs, 28–29; sign of, 17

Sporting Dog Journal, 86

Stankiewicz, Lech, 7

Stebich, Ute, *Haitian Art*, 48

Stella (author's dog), 10, 31, 37, 38, 39, 40–41, 110

Stevens, Robert (Bob), 85–109; on American pit bull terriers, 85–86, 87–88, 100–101, 108–9; ON ALTERNATIVES TO DOG FIGHTING: agility competitions, 88; conformation shows, 55, 72, 100, 102, 109; *Schutzhund*, 85, 88, 100, 102; weight-pulling competitions, 88, 102; DOGS OF: International Velvet (Velvet), 102; International Victory (Victory), 102, 103, 104, 107; Morochito, 99, 102, 103; Victory's Secret (Vickie), 102, 103; FILMS OF: *Catch Dogs and Country Living*, 86, 90; *The $100 Keep*, 100; *Japan Pit Fights*, 86, 90; *Pick-A-Winna: A Pit Bull Documentary*, 86, 90; *Pit Pro*, 100; WRITINGS OF: in *American Pit Bull Terrier Gazette*, 85; "Best Game of All," 103; *Dogs of Velvet and Steel*, 85, 95, 100, 108–9; "Let's Talk Dogs," 105; in *Pit Bull Reporter*, 98

Stevens, Wallace, "No Possum, No Sop, No Taters," 39

Stratton, Richard F., *The World of the American Pit Bull Terrier*, 82, 83

strict liability, of dog owners, 5, 6

"Suffering Dogs: The Canine Exiles from Constantinople," 115

Sura 18:22–24 (Qur'an), 157

Taşkafa (dog in Istanbul), 127, 128, 135

al-Tha'labi, Ahmad ibn Muhammad, 159, 160
Tige (Buster Brown's dog), 88
Tracey v. Solesky (2012), 5–7
Tragesser, Robert, 17
Tribe, Laurence, 93
Truffaut, François, *Jules and Jim*, 96
Turkey, animal protection in, 134–35, 174n.17
Turmunkh, Dorjkhandyn, 146, 147, 150, 175n.3
Twain, Mark, *The Innocents Abroad*, 135, 136

Ulan Bator, Mongolia, dogs in, 141–55
United Kennel Club, 77
United States v. Stevens, 87–97
U.S. Code Title 18 Section 48, 85, 91–94.
U.S. Supreme Court, on creating/ selling dog-fighting videos and other depictions of animal cruelty, 87, 88, 89, 90, 92, 96, 97

Vick, Michael, 75, 76, 87
Villarreal, Stephen C., 80
Virgil, *Aeneid*, 133

Weigel, Joseph, 6
Whitman, Walt, *Leaves of Grass*, 157–58
Wildside Kennels (North Carolina), 76
Wilkes County Animal Control (North Carolina), 76
Williams, William Carlos, *Paterson*, 116–20
Wilson, Nancy, *Yesterday's Love Songs/Today's Blue*, 33
Winston-Salem Journal, 76, 81
Wolfson, Wendy, 54, 62, 63–65

Yeats, W. B., 36

Zimmerman, Andrea Luka: *Estate, a Reverie*, 173n.3; *Taşkafa*, 123–36